Dedication

to

Harold 'Tubby' Parker

But for my late friend Tubby, there would have been no return home for me. My memory is one full of gratitude.

and

Sir Douglas Bader, CBE, DSO, DFC.

On a pleasant day in late July 1982 at the Royal Air Force museum, Hendon, I met, by arrangement, with my late Commanding Officer, Sir Douglas Bader. Together we presented the 'original' drawing of 242 Fighter Squadron's unofficial emblem for acceptance into the museum archives.

Sir Douglas and I spoke of the days spent with the squadron during the Battle of Britain. I told him a little of the fate suffered by members of the squadron after he had left them.

He repeated an earlier wish to know more. I made a promise to him that when time permitted I would write it for him. Tragically, he was not intended to read my finished account. Nevertheless, I have felt the need to complete it and pay him this tribute.

His respect and very high regard for his staff was most significant. The men of his squadron loved him for it and returned that respect twofold. He was a living example of courage and determination. Not only did he conquer his own misfortune. He also gave so many the will not only to fight on but to survive and enjoy life to the full.

THEIR
LAST TENKO

By
James Home

First published in 1989 by

Quoin Publishing Limited
The Barn
36A North Road
Kirkburton
Huddersfield
West Yorkshire HD8 0RH

© 1989 Text and photographs James Home

Printed and bound in the United Kingdom by
Netherwood Dalton & Co Limited, Huddersfield.

ISBN: 1-85563-000-1

Acknowledgements

I wish to offer a special thank you to the undermentioned who have given me invaluable help at particular stages in the story. All were 'Fepow's' (Far East Prisoners of War): Taff Simmonds, 'Copperplate' Bill, Bill Yeardye in Hamilton, Canada. My gratitude is extended to those other Fepow friends who have in one way or another helped me to complete 'our' story: Bill Griffiths, Pat McGrogan, Martin Ofield, Charlie Mantle, Tommy Orton, Geoff Lee, Ron Thompson, Dick Keefe, Joe Connor, Jack Dobson, Tom Vigurs, Bill Wakeley, Padre J N Duckworth, Syd Scales, J H W Veenstra, Eric Rice, Air Marshal Sir Harold Maguire, KCB, DSO, DFC, Air Vice Marshal Ron Ramsey-Rae, CB, OBE, Wing Commander Pitts, OBE and Sir Laurens Van Der Post. Not forgetting my non-Fepow friends who have helped along the way: Squadron Leader Hank Barlow in Calgary, Canada, Ken H Stofer in Victoria, Canada. To those kind enough to allow me the use of their own material: Air Chief Marshal Sir David Lee, KBE, GBE, CB.* Louis Allen for *End of the war in Asia*, 1979. Imperial War Museum. Public Records Office (Mr Nicholas Pointer). Press Agency (Yorkshire) Ltd. To any other person or friend whom I may have unwittingly failed to acknowledge, my most sincere thanks.
James Home (1989).

* By kind permission of the Controller of Her Majesty's Stationery Office, from *Eastwards*, 1984.

Contents

Author's Note

This story is not intended to be a historical record, for after more than forty years, I cannot say with absolute certainty that every date, place or name is correct. Many Fepow's will have their own memories still imprinted deeply on their mind; the important issue is 'our' story.

Each and every item or story used is authentic and as near to fact as is possible. In the instances where dates, places and names have not agreed, I have consulted and used official records and reports. Failing that I have opted for the consensus of opinion between those who were there. I have omitted certain surnames where it is possible that living family or friends may find it hurtful. Those names are known to me at the time of writing. Individual ranks shown may not do justice to those who later rose to higher rank, in which case I offer my apologies. The spelling of some Japanese and Malayan words are of a colloquial nature or phonetically used, for I make no claim to be linguistic.

Finally I wish to say that the story has been written with great fervour as my lifelong wish has been that our lost friends had survived '*to keep alive the spirit that kept us alive*'. Unfortunately those lives were needlessly taken.

Foreword by
Air Marshal Sir Harold Maguire,
KCB, DSO, DFC.

En route to the Far East, in the convoy to which the author refers, lectures on the area were given to the less experienced by those who had served there before. One such was given on our ship by a widely travelled army doctor. In it he said, with considerable emphasis, that if we were going to operate in the jungle we would find that casualties from tropical diseases would outnumber those caused by enemy action. Most of us with overseas experience thought he was being unduly pessimistic. Were not malaria and dysentery under control, and was not cholera a memory?

This book shows the results of an almost total withdrawal of medication combined with starvation and forced labour in a tropical environment. It is a sombre tale — but it is sadly true. I personally witnessed the initial return of some of the survivors to the Cycle camp, and the sight inside those lorries beggars description. It was the result of a deliberately evil policy by a military clique, which professed to despise those who allowed themselves to be taken prisoner, but which, when the tables were turned, almost to a man failed to take the 'honourable way'.

Some may ask, why recall this sad story so long after the events described? There are many good reasons, but the most important is that the fate of the Ambon/Haruku working parties has not yet been described in detail, and the survivors, and the families of those who died, deserve both an account and an epitaph.

1. A Vivid Memory

'Eleven, twelve, thirteen, Good God,' I found myself saying, 'that's the worst yet.'

The myopic bastards had really excelled themselves that night. As I lay weary on my uncomfortable bug-ridden bamboo shelf I found myself in some physical discomfort. Depressed and totally weary of the servitude suddenly thrust upon me I could have wept but it was not manly.

It had been another long and tortuous day — they all seemed to be in November 1943 on that small Pacific island which had the unusual name of 'Haruku'. Haruku and its adjacent island of Ambon make up part of the Muluccas group, not far from New Guinea. Each night after our labours the burials began at a place known, not very originally, as 'Boot Hill'. On that particular night number thirteen was of no superstitious significance to me; it was much worse than that, as it had meant the death of yet another close friend. It really had been a trying day — I guess they all were when you weighed in at around seven stone, feeling ill and very hungry.

Another close friend and member of our own little 'combine' of four had yesterday returned to Java. Bill was not in good shape and I was worried for him. Right then he would be on the high seas in the Jap ship *Suez Maru*. At the mercy of the Japs, storm and tempest and the Allied submarines, all I could do was pray that he would make it. Then I wondered if Bill would make it for I always had a feeling of foreboding whenever I thought of him and rumours were rife that an earlier ship had been sunk by an American sub with no survivors.

On that night I had a feeling of deep depression and self pity until I remembered I was the lucky one — just to be alive. I swore that from then on, in spite of them, I would live only for each day and hope to survive. My daily goal would be to watch every beautiful tropical sunrise and sunset until I was free of their evil bondage. To succeed I would need all the luck I could find and all the fortitude I was capable of producing from a body already showing serious signs of malnutrition and malfunction.

At *Tenko* that morning I had misjudged my latest manoeuvre to find myself an easier job; instead I landed in the most hated of working parties, in the charge of a real Jap sadist. This unfriendly guard was known as 'The Mad Monk' and he was a good one to avoid. Without the slightest justification he would lay into any prisoner with whatever weapon came readily to his itchy fingers. If he didn't like the look on your face or if the moon was new — anything was a good enough excuse to land a few heavy thumps to the face and head. It was also said that his VD condition and drug usage unbalanced any faculty he might have possessed, leading to his filthy tempers.

I had crossed him in a previous working party and until this day had successfully avoided him. Now that he had spotted me dodging around the *Tenko*

1

lines he quickly and sneeringly recruited me into his infamous party. I was no doubt scheduled to be his star turn and special guest for that day.

As I marched, or more correctly slouched, up to the drome for what seemed to be the thousandth time I allowed myself to dream of what had been. Less than two years ago, we in 242 Squadron had been a proud group whose morale had been of the highest order. Today we were far flung across the East, with many dead and others already dying for a cause that was far from clear to those of us out there. In the Far East we had experienced nothing but chaos. My innermost thoughts kept asking me 'Why do you continue to wage such an unequal battle against such odds?' I was never really sure — none of us were. Maybe there were many answers but I don't believe I ever found mine. I only know I could never stop thinking of the drastic and very frightening changes that were taking place in my life and they troubled me.

2. Journey into Chaos

It started in the sheltered harbour of Gourock on the Clyde on 8th December 1941, when we were effortlessly swept up and through two large doors of the *Empress of Australia*, a grey yet graceful looking leviathan monster. 'This is going to be a luxurious trip,' I told myself in my total ignorance.

At once my dream was shattered as an authoritative voice bawled: 'Close up ranks and stop that bloody yapping.' I thought only the good Lord himself and our top brass would know where we were heading on what was to be a most memorable day. It was a day that would live long in the memories of American people — Pearl Harbour cut deep into the pride of America.

Standing on the starboard deck I hugged the rails as the shoreline quickly slipped away from a landscape that had been unfamiliar to me. The winter darkness soon overtook us and the crowds on deck thinned out as many went below to escape the evening chill. Then the most awful news broke — news that would greatly affect our lives for the next few years and indeed would take the majority of them: 'The Japanese have bombed Pearl Harbour without even declaring war.' Was such treachery possible? Did that enemy not have a moral conscience? Many voices were heard saying: 'Where is Pearl Harbour? Is it important?'

The American Pacific fleet had been badly crippled at anchor. The battleships *Arizona* and *Oklahoma* had gone down, and six others were out of action. Three cruisers and three destroyers had been sunk or badly damaged and four hundred aircraft had been destroyed on the ground. It certainly was important.

President Roosevelt declared it a day of infamy and the USA was at war — so much for the Japanese honour, and what a way to start our cruise! Originally bound for the Middle East, we all guessed where our new destination was to be, as we, somewhat dumbstruck and alarmed at the Far East developments, changed course. The Yanks could no longer sit on the fence.

We ran into some foul weather. It was cold, damp and very misty with a heavy swell; the worst possible conditions for the many legless would-be sailors. Many were suffering badly, their bodies constantly lurching towards the nearest rails; those who hadn't eaten had nothing in their stomachs, those that had, very soon lost it. I had settled in well enough and often sat on a pile of ship's rope and watched the other ships and the movement of some mighty waves; one moment I looked at a large bank of water, the next there was nothing but the misty sky.

Days passed as the lads changed their colour like uninhibited chameleons. Then things began to look up, until one night when we were about to retire, the ship's klaxon created merry hell. It left no one in any doubt: 'Attack attack attack!' it seemed to scream.

Without further bidding, down we went, faces so close to that cold steel deck

3

that it could well have been Betty Grable down there! Then came the anti-climax and deep relief. 'False alarm,' the klaxon called. It was too late, of course, to revive some of our new members who had never experienced raids of any kind; they had already died their first death — of fright.

On about the 18th December 1941 we were given a special treat: we were invited to a film show at 7pm in the officer's mess. 'Officer's mess, where the hell's that?' came the sarcastic question.

We were told not to worry as we would be watching from the balcony. What a luxury indeed! Then came the stern warning: 'Anybody caught booing or hissing during the show will be thrown to the sharks.'

There were two films: *The Road to Singapore* and *Two Came Back*. How near the mark that ill-considered wit who chose these films came to the truth, he could never have known. No doubt his idea was born of the daily news of Jap movements which were the main topic of our conversation. We were now convinced we were bound for the Far East and communiqués became very discouraging to say the least; many would have chosen the word 'frightening'. Anyway, at about 7pm we entered the portals of the privileged, a part of the ship we had not yet seen and an area of real splendour we could not have visualised. It looked more like a scene from *Gone with the Wind* than reality, as the cigar smoke curled lazily upwards into the nostrils of the peasants.

It was the news bulletins that concerned us as the Japs walked into the Gulf of Siam ably abetted by the Vichy French. The Japs were probing in and around Hong Kong, both from the mainland and from Formosa in the South China Sea. The whole of the Malayan archipelago was now within easy reach from the Philippines right down to the Dutch East Indies. Indeed, the northernmost provinces of Australia would be at serious risk. But we were told: 'Don't worry, the myopic bandy-legged bastards could never find a way past the fortress of Singapore.' Singapore, the bastion of the East. That word, bastion, would soon become a dirty word, even an obscenity, as the fingers of fate, unknown to us, were fast spreading over the convoy and our lives. 'Churchill's gift to Nippon' is how we would later be described and fate would deal many savage blows upon many untrained, unarmed, and even less prepared men in that convoy, culminating in the horrific tragedies of the Far East prisoner of war camps.

We had been at sea for more than fourteen days with Christmas only a few days away. The sea was like a millpond whilst the sun warmed and sparkled on each crest of a wave. On 24th December we awakened to find ourselves at anchor off the port of Freetown on the north-western coast of Africa. There was no breeze to fan the brow, the sky was hazy in the shimmering heat and the sea was like a sheet of glass. Stretching limitlessly around us the land mass looked absolutely colourless. When the hot sun sank beneath the horizon it brought very little relief as the air stayed stagnant and oppressive. We lazed away Christmas Day of 1941 in this almost breathless environment.

The next day we left unheralded, in the same way as we had arrived, only to hear yet more shattering news. Hong Kong had fallen and all the garrison had been taken prisoner. Rumour was rife about the Japanese atrocities in the colony, about the needless bayoneting and other harsh demeaning treatment of the indigenous population. The myth of an invincible Nippon was gaining credence in the minds of many and we wondered what the devil was happening, and why we were being sent at this late hour, ill-equipped and not trained to fight as infantry, unlike our soldier comrades.

The prospects were not good even for the optimists amongst us and the consensus of opinion was that we would arrive some three months late. As though to fortify our sagging morale and to grant us some conviction of our own invincibility along came HMS *Ramillies*. She was a magnificent spectacle to those of us who had not been so close to a battleship before, her bows cleaving through the calm blue sea, her large guns pointing fore and aft, and her superstructure rising majestically toward the sky. She was making about five knots more headway than the convoy as she checked the ships within her care. All too soon, she disappeared to her station, having made her contacts with the other ships. The parting signal of the *Ramillies* was: 'I am returning to base, we wish you all well, good luck.' They should have added, 'You'll need it.'

The *Ramillies* was not deserting us in our hour of need, however, for the *Royal Sovereign* took over, bringing more ships from the Middle East and swelling the gift to Nippon even more. I was never sure if the size of that convoy was supposed to frighten the Japs but it certainly looked like a force to be reckoned with.

It was quite pleasant lying on deck at night looking at the myriad of stars which studded the heavens — sometimes the effect could be quite disorientating if one fixed one's gaze on a particular star. Whenever there was a slight swell, it was as though the whole firmament was sweeping past then it would seem to rush back again until that same star reappeared. Your mind's eye seemed to tell you that you were actually on the move yourself. Laying there it seemed to become a private battle of mind over matter until finally your eyes closed for the night.

By the time we were twelve days out of Sierra Leone, still heading steadily south, speculation was high and hopes were being pinned on a landfall in South Africa — hopes that were fortified by knowing nods from the crewmen.

On 8th January 1942 we were faced with a most wondrous sight as we arrived outside Cape Town. A magnificent panorama stretched out before us: a clear blue sea splashed with green, with the land providing a backcloth of dwellings tiled in red with white walls. Only one other thing could have surpassed so much beauty, and there it was — Table Mountain. It was an awe inspiring sight, with its steeply rising slopes culminating in a huge plateau. There was neither depression nor pinnacle to distract from its flatness — truly remarkable. This, I told myself, had to be paradise and we should make the most of everything on offer. It was indeed a land of honey and for ourselves an all too brief escape from reality.

The ship's rails were crowded as we all stood riveted and gazing incredulously at the landfall before our eyes. It had come exactly when we needed it most. News travelled quickly telling us that we were to be paid in the morning, then allowed on shore. But first there was a short talk on a code of behaviour, followed by advice on how to avoid the scourge of VD which scared the life out of we younger ones. Coloured people were denied certain facilities but this was a discrimination that did not fully register as being of importance, for everyone seemed most contented with their lot at that moment in time. We were more concerned with our new-found environs.

Soon we were alongside the quay, our hawsers dropped then slipped over the capstans by a team of black South Africans whose bodies gleamed in the sunlight. The huge doors of our ship opened and a large gangway was secured. As we left the ship my attention was drawn to the cavalcade of cars assembled on the quayside. There were dozens, mostly chauffeured by coloureds resplendent in their smart uniforms and with wide grins on their faces. I remember wondering what they were doing there. The majority of cars were large American Chevrolets, De-Soto, Pontiac, Oldsmobiles and Fords. I then noticed that as the smartly dressed men left the ship they were called into parties of four or five and whisked away. Some did not wish to join a party preferring to seek out the local hostelries.

Four of us climbed aboard a Chevrolet and off we went not knowing to whom or where and caring even less. The chauffeur began to speak to us and explained his programme — the car belonged to a rich lady who owned a local estate just outside the town. We were to be driven to some of the more outlandish and important sights of interest in areas not conveniently reached by public transport and we were to relax in luxury — something we did not find difficult. Our driver pointed out the landmarks and every roadside seemed to be landscaped with the most beautiful tropical shrubs and flowers. It was delightful.

We came upon our first stop and climbed out to admire the view overlooking the Cape Peninsular, then continued along mountain roads. Suddenly we reached the Cecil Rhodes monument high upon the Cape — a splendid edifice and a very worthy tribute to a Britisher. Then on again to view the bas-relief of the 'Volk Trekkers', the Boer farmers who in 1836 migrated from the Cape to the Transvaal. This huge bas-relief depicted in detail prairie-type wagons drawn by many oxen, and the Boer families transporting all their worldly possessions into the hinterland.

Off we sped again on this wondrous tour — the Japs might well have been centuries away for all we cared. This dear old lady was doing a fine job. Without further notice we entered a huge estate with its palatial residence, a fine white building very reminiscent of the country houses in the Southern States of America. There she was, sitting so supreme at her table on the lawn, a gracious looking lady, every inch a dowager. She stood to greet us and talked benevolently to us each in turn, asking about our respective backgrounds. A grand, though light, meal was served with cold iced drinks to suit the most pernickety of palates whilst we talked about the views we had seen and thanked the lady for her kindness. Waving away our thanks she said it was the very least she could do for the British boys from back home. 'Joseph,' she said to the chauffeur, 'don't forget to show the boys the view off the point where the Atlantic embraces the Indian Ocean.'

Off we went again with Joseph in charge duly arriving at the headland to view the meeting of those two oceans before returning to town. Joseph continued to the docks for more passengers. We certainly had forgotten for a while the trials and tribulations that were soon to be upon us; there was not an inkling of the turmoil to the East, nor the dreary blacked-out land of England we had left behind barely a month before.

My good friend Dick Keefe, who had a remarkably good tenor voice, had been making guest appearances at the Alhambra Theatre for the duration of our stay, and we had seen the unique and interesting Del Monti nightclub with its ceiling that opened outwards to the starry sky. Our *Empress* looked so lovely at night all lit up, yet she could not match the sleek *Warwick Castle* which lay alongside us. After four or five days we lined the rails once more to say a grateful good-bye and thank you to Cape Town. The Table Mountain was shrouded in a heavy mist — we were most fortunate to see this 'tablecloth' on the mountain as it is a phenomenon displayed only at irregular intervals.

We now joined more ships from the Middle East including our sister ship *Empress of Asia* and the *City of Canterbury, Felix Roussel* and I believe the *Andes.*

On about 16th January we knew the possible destination had to be Singapore and we thought 'May God help us.'

Gossip turned once again to the conflict which came nearer with the passing of each day. The strength of the enemy forces making rapid advances were surprising many and frightening a few. The Japs enhanced the myth of their invincibility as their steam-roller tactics appeared determined to crush all resistance encountered. The reported treatment of those defeated peoples sent shivers down our spines.

At the time of their disgraceful attack on Pearl Harbour, the Japs had landed troops on French Indo-China on the pretext of protecting that country from the French and British. Landings were made on the east coast of the Malayan peninsular and at Luzon in the Philippines, between 15th of December and Christmas Day, they attacked and took Hong Kong. On 17th December 1941 the Japs had landed on North Borneo and on the 24th they landed at Kuching in Sarawak. They had made good progress through the so-called impenetrable jungle of Malaysia on cycles and in primitive armoured vehicles. The tin and rubber industries together with the oil wells of Borneo were faced with impending loss. By now the Japs were established on the islands of New Guinea and the Solomons not too far from the shores of Australia. In North Malaya they were making inroads as they pushed north through Rangoon and up toward Mandalay where opposition was even lighter.

The Royal Navy had suffered the ignomy of losing in one go the HMS *Prince of Wales* and the *Repulse*, a most serious and crippling blow and perhaps the turning point of the campaign. The Navy were left with only a number of light cruisers and some destroyers including those of Holland and Australia. That light force put up a valiant fight to stem the tide of Jap invasions throughout the East, but unfortunately their strength could not match a strong and efficient enemy naval force which included a force of aircraft carriers. We also heard of the invasion of the Aleutian islands; it seemed the enemy had a foot in every door which was unnerving the inhabitants throughout the Pacific. They were also threatening India by way of Burma.

Still we steamed eastwards until one morning late in January landfall was sighted and we appeared to be heading for a channel between what were identified as Sumatra and Java; the channel was the Sunda Straits. As we entered the Straits we enjoyed the first of many sights we would long remember. She stood there graceful yet all powerful, gaunt yet majestic in her beauty and a symbol of great strength. She was *Krakatau*, sentinel of the Sunda Straits and still volcanic. She seemed to rise and threaten to spew her red hot lava at the first sign of interference, perhaps nature's way of saying 'Lay your hands on me at your peril'.

It now seemed that the final decision had been taken and three or four ships were to try for entry into Singapore's Keppal harbour. With the Japs almost at Singapore Island it was thought unwise to risk sending more ships. However, the *Empress of Asia, City of Canterbury, Felix Roussel* and the *Andes*, carrying fighting troops and essential supplies, were to make this risky attempt. The *City of Canterbury* zig-zagged her way into port under an umbrella of Japanese bombers and remarkably she avoided direct hits, though some men were wounded by shrapnel from near misses. The *Empress of Asia*, bringing brigades of the 18th Division from Bombay, was hit and set on fire; she was hit early on in the attack and was burning throughout her entire length. The ship was then beached on a sand bar whilst naval destroyers lifted many men off; others were in the water for five or six hours with some losses. The *Felix Roussel* carried troops of the Northumberland Fusiliers and was defended by their own Vickers machine-gunners; their guns were lashed to whatever good fixing could be found. The remaining personnel placed themselves in any decent rifle position at vantage points on the top deck. This action of the NF's went a long way towards keeping their attackers at a safer height whilst she made headway into the relative safety of Keppal harbour. The *Felix* had three square funnels, one of which I believe was false, and one of which received a bomb directly down it — it was a most unusual looking French ship!

We on the *Empress of Australia* continued through the Sunda Straits sailing very close to the shoreline, so close in fact, that our wash actually appeared to flood over the very low coastline. 'My God what a place to be ambushed,' was the concerned expression of many as we negotiated the narrow channel. Suddenly we found ourselves in a large basin at the entrance to a dock — Tandjoeng Priok, Batavia (now Djkarta), capital of Java.

As we moved in, there were other liners moving out loaded with women and children who cheered us at their loudest, possibly cheers of sympathy. Little did they know that a large Jap fleet was just one obstacle they would need to overcome if they were ever to reach home. Most of those women and children were already doomed to be blown out of the water to be killed or drowned within the hour.

The *Empress* not only got herself stuck on a sandbar but was also subjected to a false air raid alarm before we disembarked. We entered the city limits along wide roads thronged on both sides by cheering locals who jumped up and down waving frantically and shouting in their native tongue. We had to assume that it was a welcome — if it was, then it certainly did not last very long. Hundreds of cyclists weaved in and out, some moving nonchalantly along as though without a care in this world or the next. Our journey continued until we reached the heart of Batavia which looked very attractive, well laid out, spacious and very clean, somewhat reminiscent of Cape Town. Cars flashed by until we turned off into the grounds of King Wilhelm III School. It was really good to be on terra firma once more albeit some seven thousand miles from dear old Blighty.

After settling in, we were paid about £2.10 (in Dutch Guilders) and let loose on the unsuspecting town. Outside the gates we hopped onto an electric tram. Knowing no better we had boarded the rear car and found ourselves in with the coloureds. The conductor looked really non-plussed by our presence and only then did we realise the Dutch were practising their own brand of segregation. Selecting a likely looking spot we left the tram and so avoided a revolution.

There was no shortage of lights; apparently no one yet understood the meaning of a black-out despite the near proximity of conflict. There was still a normal active nightlife with shades of Singapore and the *Tuan Besar*. After a look around, a drink and meal of fried rice with all the celebrated trimmings of the Dutch lifestyle it was back to school. But not before the trishaw rider had tried his hardest to take us for a final course of '*Mak mak*'. This time the dish was not rice but his beautiful sister, according to him. Apparently this was a common enough practice especially when the girl was saving for her bottom drawer and no one seemed too upset by it. Fortunately we were almost at the school before the gesticulations were fully understood by we innocents, otherwise we may have lost someone!

The following day after breakfast we were taken out to the civil airfield where we unpacked wooden crates which had been brought from the *Empress* and other ships. The crates held our tools and some spare parts for the Hurricanes we had yet to see. Other lads from 242 Squadron had gone to the docks of Tandjoeng Priok to unload unassembled Hurricanes which were still in the crates; all we needed was time to service them so someone would need to tell *Dai Nippon* to hang on. During the next few days this job was given top priority. Then came a further surprise as 242 Squadron was split into two sections; one half would be moving to Sumatra, the other would remain in Java. Our destination was to be Palembang which stood alongside the river Moesi. The airstrips were known as P1 and P2, the former being north of the town, the latter a secret field to the south of town. Neither Sumatra nor Java had yet come under the tyrants heel, although it did look imminent. On 21st January 1942 the Japs had landed on Balikpapen, Borneo, and Ambon had fallen on the 31st. On 6 February those selected were driven to the nearby station to await a train to begin a trek into the dense jungle land of Sumatra.

During our stay in Batavia my friends and I had fallen in love with what we had seen, not least the beautiful tanned Dutch girls. The people of Java, at all social levels, seemed as if they had been a happy enough people before all the outsiders interfered in their business. Native life was totally unaffected, or so it seemed, by the trappings of our so-called civilisation and modern day progress. The women at work were, in our eyes, very picturesque with their jet black hair tied in the inevitable bun, barefoot and clad only in a very colourful sarong wrapped around the breasts and tucked in.

My reminiscing ended abruptly when the train approached, pulled by a small puffing and steaming locomotive. We climbed aboard for the next stage of the mystery trip, this this time hoping the enemy would not arrive ahead of us. It was the 9th February, the day after the Japs made their land attack on Singapore on Sunday the 8th. It seemed they had established a pattern begun at Pearl Harbour to hit their Western defenders on a Sunday. After all, no self-respecting Christians would expect their enemy to do battle on the Sabbath. The same pattern of strikes in various territories was repeated time and again on a scale that became almost monotonous.

The train rolled on through the countryside. On one side a secondary jungle with *kampongs* (native villages) often came into view, and the next minute it was a landscape of thick undergrowth. Slowly the train came to its first halt and appearing as though from nowhere came hordes of noisy natives onto the track sidings. No, we were not being ambushed, but were about to be conned. Their only weapons were fruit and other foods; they had brought brown sugar cakes, fish cakes, bananas, fried bananas (*pisang goring*) and endless other tasty morsels. Brisk trading took place whilst the engine took on wood and water. Soon we were on our way westwards. Before long the coast was spotted and a small harbour which would be Merak.

Disembarking from the train we boarded a small KLM ferry then headed out across the Sunda Straits. Small islands were dotted everywhere: low ones with little topography; others with a beach approach; many more with small cliffs and rocks; and dense undergrowth on some — they were all a joy to see. We chugged along for a few hours dodging in and out of the islands which held the steady interest of most. No doubt the lads were wondering what really did lay around the next corner although no one wished to sound or appear concerned.

Finally we arrived at the Southern tip of Sumatra, at the port of Oosthaven, with our old friend *Krakatau* not too far away watching our every movement.

That volcano, some 600 feet high out of the water, was a powerful reminder of the 1883 eruption which had terminated in a fifty-foot tidal wave which caused the deaths of some 36,000 Indonesians. My first and almost last memory of Oosthaven, a dense jungle spot, was the almost thunderous chatter of a thousand monkeys. It was echoed by an equal number of throaty roars from the largest bull-frogs ever seen. Someone did remark that the film *Bring Them Back Alive* had been shot in Sumatra which I did not doubt. I only hoped that our little lot would be brought out alive. Being no Tarzan and without my Jane I saw no good reason to venture into the wild and dense jungle. I stayed close to the water's edge, then my mine wandered to sharks and crocodiles so I move into no-man's land somewhere between the two.

The train now had a good head of steam as it stood puffing and blowing, spewing out dirty wood smoke into the clear blue sky. It was most probably a second or even third class train with its slatted hard wood seating in dingy overcrowded coaches. Moving northwards toward Palembang we flitted in and out of many cuttings, one minute in the beautiful sunlight, the next in the darkest jungle. The countryside was so unlike Java, cold and dank in dense places, almost to the point of foreboding. There were not many *kampongs* to be seen through the dense undergrowth to relieve our monotony.

The train steamed ahead like a writhing snake in its homely environs stopping only to replenish itself with food and water. As we moved through that hostile terrain we were developing an intense dislike for Sumatra which was not a bit like home. At last the train pulled into Palembang and we made our way to the place of our accommodation, once more a school building. It was here on the small grassed paddock that my two best friends at that time had their battle *royale*. Johnny Smith, Percy Heath and myself made ourselves comfortable in those strange surroundings. No one had taken any sleep whilst travelling and most felt rather tired and restless which caused words between my two friends and words led to blows which finished on the grass as a battle. Bravely, for both were bigger than me, I got between them and stayed there until they cooled off — a memorable beginning.

On 2 February 1942, approximately forty Hurricanes arrived from various points onto the airfield of P1 ten miles north of Palembang. If that was to be our full complement of fighters it was not going to take us very far. The pilots were from 232 and 258 Squadrons; later they would combine with 242 and 605 to form a new wing numbered 226. Additionally, a number of Brewster Buffaloes (fighter planes) arrived but were never put into action, being considered unsuitable — a great help!

Our first night in Palembang found our adjutant enquiring into the current position and seeking orders. The accommodation at P1 was almost non-existent so it was decided only essential personnel would go to the airstrip. It was generally considered that P1 would present us with our first confrontation with the great *Dai Nippon* in one form or another.

3. East meets West

It was 10th February 1942 and we had spent the first night sleeping as usual on stone floors in Palembang school. Air Commodore Vincent, DFC, AFC, tells us the following in his history of No 226 group.

10.1.42   Air Commodore Vincent was informed by telephone at 2300 hours that he might be required to proceed to the Far East immediately.

11.1.42   Posting was confirmed and instructions were issued to leave by air in four days time.

12.1.42   Air Commodore Vincent informed that he would command a fighter group of eight squadrons, and that Air Commodore J Hunter would proceed at the same time to command a bomber group, both Headquarters Far East Command.

18.1.42   Proceeded from Plymouth by *Cattalina* with Air Marshal Sir Richard Pierse, Air Commodore Williams, Air Commodore Hunter and Squadron Leader Wilson.

28.1.42   Arrived Singapore and reported to Air Vice Marshal Pulford who informed Air Commodore Vincent that 'no information had been received, that he was arriving and that there was no job for him'. As 224 Group was already functioning in Singapore, a change at that critical stage was not desirable.

1.2.42   In consequence of the retirement of the British Forces to Singapore Island, the heavy air raids on the four aerodromes and the proximity of Seletar to the mainland and the probability of shelling, Air Commodore Vincent was instructed to proceed to Palembang in Sumatra to form a new fighter group, No 226, from squadrons evacuated from Singapore and from the groundstaffs of No 266 Group.

2.2.42   Approximately forty Hurricanes arrived at P1 with 232 and 258 Squadrons. Accommodation at P1 was non-existent; no cooking facilities, and no dispersal huts or water laid on. There was no heavy ack ack and very few slit trenches and its defence consisted of four Bofor guns and a handful of Dutch troops. There was a complete lack of transport. The position improved slightly but there were substantial deficiencies throughout the operations in both Sumatra and Java. It was extremely difficult for groundstaff between Palembang and the airfield of P1. Vehicles were not available to convey personnel to their defence posts. This seriously affected the defence of P1 when it was later attacked by paratroops. There was one poor telephone line between Palembang and the duty pilot, nothing at dispersal points and there was no equipment to upgrade them. RT to aircraft was most unsatisfactory, the transmitter being a considerable distance away and messages had to be relayed by telephone, sometimes by a Dutchman who was unaccustomed to the work. In short, valuable communications were totally inadequate and almost non-existent. Hurricane tools, apart from those brought by No 266 wing, were not available. Supplies of aircraft spares and ammunition were not available, nor were battery charging facilities or battery trolleys. No 258 Squadron were first serviced by Buffalo crews. All this contributed to a low state of serviceability. The majority of the pilots were straight from OTU and with the exception of the CO's and two or three Flight Commanders, all pilots were completely inexperienced operationally: for example twenty-two pilots out of twenty-six in one squadron had no operational experience at all. No 266 Group (including 242 and 605 groundstaffs) therefore started its existence extremely ill-equipped.

The History of No 226 Group says that on 11th February Group Headquarters staff, together with ground personnel of 242, 258 and 605 with wing signals, arrived from Batavia and were addressed by Air Commodore Vincent. The general bearing and morale of these troops was excellent and considerably cheered the ground personnel who had come from Malaya and Singapore with very low morale — a number of them were failing to stand up to the bombing and aircraft were not being immediately refuelled and re-armed during raids . . .

That then is how we were received into Palembang and onto P1 airfield — not the most satisfactory proposition for a great deal of optimism. Before we had arrived at the airfield it had already been attacked on a number of occasions and the pilots had already been very busy on sorties over Singapore. Not many of the groundstaff had rifles or any other firearms except, of course, the squadron's RAF regiment lads. Those of 605 provided the labour at P1 to dig many more slit trenches and improve defences any way they could. The airfield was previously a civilian airstrip used mainly by the Dutch airline KLM. It had two runways, the main one being about 1200 metres long.

Our strength in every respect was absolutely abysmal which was a great pity (or mistake), for Sumatra should have been a very sharp thorn in the enemy's side. The Japs should have found Sumatra a different proposition to any that they had so far conquered, with its east coast unbroken for some seven hundred miles from its southernmost tip and with swampland covering seventy miles inland from its coast. When the swampland gave way it was only to jungle with yet more swamps, wild animals, snakes and all kinds of associated pestilence. Given reasonable back-up of air strength and battle-hardened pilots and crews with their proper equipment, there could have been a different story to tell. The real jungle could have swallowed the enemy armies, for the terrain would have been our best ally. As it was they had to use the river Moesi to bring in their troops in a very exposed situation. Yet in the little time given, the pilots of 232 and 258 had slaughtered the majority by simply strafing unprotected small boats. The Japs were given command of the skies; they did not have to win it and that was the only reason they had come so far, according to those who were there. It is indeed a salutary thought that with another hundred Hurricanes and pilots, it might well have been a totally different story in that theatre of the Far East war.

The school we slept in had several rooms with tiled floors and louvered windows, and a patio surrounded the building. About ten yards from that patio was a stream, its flow only just perceptible. Local natives using the stream chattered away and washed their clothing whilst taking a great deal of notice of our comings and goings. Apparently most friendly, we were warned that they were probably counting and calculating strengths for the benefit of their new-found 'liberators'.

Early on the morning of 11th February, the senior NCO's called a parade at which point our officers arrived. Our acting CO, affectionately known as 'John Willie', was in fact our adjutant, the second officer being FO Power of our squadron regiment. John Willie gave us a nice little pep talk during which he told us: 'Look here lads, we are going to stop these ******* s' — an indication of how well someone had briefed him at his earlier meeting!

I had been instructed to take guard with two others on the nearby road which led to P1 airfield. My first questions were 'What do these Japs look like? How are they different from the local Chinese?' I remember there being no rush to answer my questions for it seemed many others were non too sure. I had only seen the occasional Jap when I had visited the docks at Middlesbrough during my school-days. I could not imagine the differences between the many native Chinese or any other of the many Asiatics that may have come along. It was a wierd experience taking guard duty in those circumstances; perhaps in reality it was just a little frightening or at least off-putting. I wouldn't have been surprised to be told I had let all of their 5th Column through, believing them to be Sumatrans — we just did not have a clue.

On 11th February a party of mainly fitters was chosen to go to P1 for servicing duties, whilst the rest spent their time idling about the schoolhouse. When the lads came back in the evening they told us of the current position. To say they were appalled would be a grave understatement — they claimed the pilots were having a really tough time, and were not being looked after as they had the right to expect. Apparently B17's (Flying Fortress's) had been using the grassed runways and now they were deeply rutted making it that much more difficult for Hurricane pilots to take off and land.

With the lads back from the drome, we decided to have a quick look in the town of Palembang. Arriving at the river's edge, we found a flat-bottomed raft-like ferry waiting to take passengers across the river; a most peculiar crossing. We had noticed how fast flowing the river currents were but thought nothing about them as the ferry left the nearside bank. Those currents immediately took hold of the ferry carrying it in the wrong direction as it sped down river still on the same side from which we had boarded.'What a bloody awful driver,' someone suggested. As it moved swiftly along, it very, very, slowly gained distance towards the centre of the river. When it had reached about half-way across, it hit equally fast currents going in the opposite direction. We were then taken the same distance back whilst slowly going forward to find ourselves spot on at the other side. Perfect navigation which could only have resulted from an intimate knowledge of River Moesi and its currents.

The town of Palembang was straight and narrow, best described as a western 'one horse (street) town' with plenty of native-style shops and one very small cinema, the Luxor. We found the usual cafe which supplied us with those well-flavoured drinks we had obtained in Batavia. With not much to see because it only really served the nearby oil installation at Pladjoe, our brief sojourn ended.

Thursday 12th February brought me my first sighting of P1 airfield. Johnny and Percy had already gone with some of their RAF Regiment pals and their officer,

Chris Power. They had all gone to take up their defence duties on the airfield which would keep them rather busy and I would not see my friends again until after the action which was to follow.

A few 242 Squadron groundstaff who still retained their rifles (myself included) were instructed to join up with the regiment lads of either squadron should the services of our own trades not be required. First, I was to help out on the improvement of telecommunications and radio links by investigating the battery position and telephone lines — or rather the lack of both. If possible I was to set up a battery charging room. My first findings were that the reports given to us were certainly not over-stated, in fact the opposite. This situation was, to say the very least, scandalous on an airfield in a known theatre of war: one telephone link with an observer post; no battery trolleys; and all other batteries in a badly run down condition. Improvements other than very minor ones required equipment. Even then it would be impossible time-wise to bring the position anywhere near to RAF standard. It was pathetic, a certain sign that it was never intended to realistically defend the airfield, and it should be remembered that the British were not in overall command of the defence.

Thursday 12th and also Friday 13th saw everyone working hard to improve the overall situation by servicing aircraft and generally digging slit trenches — there were no demarcation lines for rank or trade. Happily the morale of 242 and 605 groundstaffs was still excellent, most of us still enjoying our new experiences and excitement, with not enough time to worry too much of the eventual outcome. Within an hour of our arrival at P1 on the Friday, it all began to liven up. We were visited by seven or eight bombers and some thirty or so fighters, who at once proceeded to strafe the airfield. Fortunately we were not strangers to this lack of hospitality; in France and during the Battle of Britain we had matured very early on. Unfortunately, on this occasion a number of lads were killed and others were injured, all from 605 Squadron. 242 Squadron had no casualties that day.

Little did we know as we busied ourselves that by the 15th the enemy would have captured every conceivable land mass in the area except for Sumatra and Java. On Saturday 14th February, we did not even suspect the shocks that lay in store for us. At about 0830 hours, the new slightly-improved observer system reported a large bomber force approaching from the north. To the best of my knowledge, the airmen on the field received no warning except for a red flag that was flown but seen by few. At first no one was too concerned as the planes were easily recognised as Hudsons: we were even grateful for this relief force and some were preparing to cheer them in. That was until a number of light bombs began to fall on and around the airfield. 'You stupid buggers, we are not bloody Japs' is a watered down version of the reception they received.

We still believed that they had made the mistake of thinking our airfield was already in Jap hands. Worse still, all our Hurricanes had only just taken off — it was as though someone had just told the bomber force. As the bombers made their turn and a second pass with the bomb doors open, the sky filled with falling bodies as white and orange parachutes slowly floated down. Had their height not been so great and the ground defence guns not lowered their sights to near ground level, they would have scored a bullseye. As it was, they had to swing away for their own safety. There would have been nothing to stop them had they made the airfield, except our miserable collection of rifles and the four Bofor guns. We would have been no competition for what was certainly a crack unit of fearless fighters, or as some rumoured, the released murderers from Japan's prisons. The paratroops, some 250, made ground around the outside of the airfield perimeter, and another 100 were dropped to attack the nearby oil installation of Pladjoe, about four miles downriver.

The History of No 226 Group says: " . . . at this time all serviceable Hurricanes were away on escort of a bomber force proceeding to attack enemy transport in the Banka Straits off the mouth of River Moesi. Immediately it occurred, attempts were made to recall the fighters but contact could not be made by RT because the distance was too great. On their return the pilots were given what warning was possible and the majority landed on P2 (secret strip). All available armed personnel were at once rushed to P1 from Palembang to engage the enemy. Owing to the shortage of small arms, a large number of personnel on the airfield were unarmed. During the day they were evacuated through the enemy lines back to Palembang . . ."

Despite sniping, RAF groundstaff had managed to get through to the airfield and the 3.7 guns and the Bofors were successfully withdrawn to new positions with some casualties. There were two Welsh ack-ack units, one was possibly the 77th heavy, and they tried shooting at treetop level once the Japanese parachutists were sighted. Not many were shot down but they were forced to re-direct themselves away from the airfield and into the jungle which was in its way a great success. The majority of Japs finished up between the airfield and the town of Palembang.

Then confusion arose. Apparently the Dutch forces had no plan for defence — we had only seen one coloured army group whom I thought were Ambonese and I had seen very few white Dutch soldiers. Word was reaching us of men being attacked on the road back to Palembang as they attempted to return to the town as instructed. By afternoon the CO, Wing Commander Maguire, instructed all service groundstaff who were not required to make their own break out from the airfield. If they reached Palembang unharmed they were to move on to P2 on their way out to Oosthaven, and give what help was required of them at P2. This left on P1 only the RAF Regiment lads and some armed groundstaff with a couple of ancient machine guns and Ross or Lee Enfield rifles.

I believe many of those lads who tried to reach Palembang were killed in ambush and face to face confrontation with the enemy. One of the two RAF Regiment officers, an Irishman, had taken charge of our party whilst our own officer, Chris Power, and my friends, Johnny and Percy, had gone into the jungle on demolition work. Although a number of parachutists had been killed, by midday they had re-grouped and consolidated to hold the main road, about three quarters of a mile south of P1 and north of a road block. The road was apparently jammed with lorries which had been ambushed and overturned on their way to the airfield. Further unsuccessful attempts were made during the day to reach P1 with reinforcements of food and water, both of which were always short.

Repeated to no avail were requests to the Dutch to force a way through for us with their armoured cars. At about 1650 hours a company of Ambonese soldiers armed with mortars and machine guns arrived at the road block and commenced to advance along the road. They soon returned with their Dutch Commander who said that it would be impossible to clear the road until daylight the following morning.

There was no way that our paratroop combatants would close down for the night to oblige that commander — in fact it was just what the Japs were hoping for. On P1 after the army guns had made their way to new positions, 'all' men (ie unarmed) were given a final opportunity to attempt getting back to Palembang on foot — there was no spare transport. The alternative was to stay with the more experienced regiment lads which one or two did; they drove the vehicles and generally helped out. I sincerely believe the officers we had were a strong influence on all those who volunteered to stay back; in particular, the Wing Commander.

This is how my exit with the majority of 605 Squadron regiment men and a few groundstaff of both 242 and 258 is remembered. By mid-afternoon the CO had gathered all remaining armed men together in the control building to one side of the airfield. From there we had an open airfield on one side and, as far as we knew, the Japs on two flanks. On the fourth side was a rather wide and well-trodden path, certainly wide enough to take a lorry, which ran in the general direction of the north towards the main road running between Djambi and Palembang. At about 1730 hours we thought we were in luck, as a party of unidentified soldiers moved towards the control building — they would be a great help to us on our way out. Suddenly, one of the Ambonese with us who was using binoculars screamed wildly: 'Yapan, Yapan soldat!'

We opened fire in their general direction after which our Irish officer went out to investigate. For some reason they had simply melted away. That was my first real taste of front line action. There was a short lull in proceedings, during which time we suspected the enemy outside were setting us up — our stomachs were full of butterflies! With a commanding view we could hold out on all sides except one as long as the ammo lasted and we weren't overwhelmed by a force of numbers. About ten of us were instructed to destroy all unserviceable aircraft and plant at the so-called dispersal points. Having completed that destruction we returned to find that the second regiment officer had joined us with about ten men. They had apparently been opposing the enemy on the Palembang road, assisting others to get out, and were now returning to join their CO, Wing Commander Maguire, and the rest of us. There was a limited reserve of ammunition other than that held by each man which had been brought in from a shed on the edge of the field. Any action around and on the drome had substantially quietened and the dangers appeared less although still of some concern.

At about 1800 hours the CO decided that the fifty or so of us must get out before the enemy re-formed and attacked the building which was possibly their final obstacle. There was no question of surrender — I doubt if anyone dared mention the word in the CO's presence. In any case the enemy would be taking no prisoners, except to let their blood flow fast and red — the way they liked it. Also, there was no way anyone would trust the enemy's Pearl Harbour style of honour.

The CO decided to do a short reconnoitre outside before the action. Then an amazing thing happened which I cannot remember in full detail: the CO and another officer went out and bumped into a small party of Japs who must have been as shocked as the CO for no one instantly opened fire. Our CO made an instant decision to bluff it out and asked for their *shoko* (officer) who then offered Wing Commander Maguire and ourselves a safe passage into Palembang. Neither side knew the strength of the other so were able to parley, each with a pretence of strength. Thinking quickly, our CO told the Jap that he must first discuss the offer with his superior who lay wounded in our building — surprisingly this was accepted. We now had to move out quickly and it was about 6.30pm when three officers and about fifty to sixty airmen boarded our three lorries and headed north-west. The Jap party must have also been unsure for they had melted away instead of opening fire on us.

We were on a road which ran north toward Djambi. Somehow we hoped to find a way back south-west towards P2 airfield. Our first stop was at a plantation of rubber trees. I imagine the stop was for us to stretch our legs and seek any useful geographical information. We spoke to some people who eventually joined our convoy, which was still heading north-west. Our next stop, apart from changing drivers from time to time, was, I think, to cross the River Moesi to its south side. Another stop was made at a native *kampong* where, for some unknown reason, the natives became quite belligerent toward us. It was assumed that in some way they had connections with the enemy, maybe 5th Column or simply sympathisers. It was decided to post guards on shifts throughout the night whilst the rest of us dozed on the vehicles.

Into the second day which was about the 16th February, we changed our general direction from north-west to south-west. It seemed that Padang offered no way out. The CO must have been acting on information received at one of the stops we had made. We had travelled a most uncomfortable 250-300 miles when it was decided to head for a port named Bencolen. It was now being said that if Bencolen offered us no escape route we would have to head direct for P2 and Oosthaven, travelling as close to the west coast as possible, hoping to find petrol along the way.

Though tired and full of apprehension, this part of our journey is easy to remember. The sheer ruggedness and dominating scenery of a most beautiful and huge mountain range made it almost possible to forget our predicament. Sensing that freedom may have been short-lived we soaked up the warmth and serenity for many more miles; battle could have been a million miles away or just around the next corner. If only time could have stood still until 1945.

Before we finally arrived at Bencolen, concern was expressed about the reaction we would receive from those living in this small port. One lorry and its men was held back a mile or two outside the port to guard our rear. At this time I remember feeling quite proud of the discipline and efficiency of our small, well-led party. In Bencolen arrangements were easily made to board what proved to be the last small ship to leave the port as we headed for Java. All our actions and the foresight and leadership of Wing Commander Maguire, ably assisted by everyone, proved to be our immediate salvation. The only concern about leaving from Bencolen was that we had to make the sea journey on a light night. We had to pray that the Jap fleet was not straddled across our path, waiting to pounce on any stray vessel.

We finally docked at Tjilatjap, which lies at the western end of Java where the Sunda Straits meet the Indian Ocean. All was well and we had made it — into another chaotic trap. By train we travelled into Batavia (Djkarta) and joined our respective units. Squadrons 242 and 605 had already settled in and were operating from the airfield of Tjililitan with the pilots of 258 and 232. Our Sumatran exercise had been an experience and had thankfully ended well. For the moment we were grateful — but for what, I was about to wonder. All the 242 staff were accounted for except Johnny and Percy, together with their officer, Chris Power. I was preparing to mourn them when, three days later, in walked the three of them. After many problems they had found a way out through Oosthaven.

February 18th 1942 dawned in its usual glorious way with mosquitos droning back into their dark and dank quarters like a million dracula's preparing their next evening's attack. Already we had noticed how often the Japs made their strikes on a Sunday, sticking to a rigid pattern so easy to read. This was a lesson that would be turned to the Allies' advantage later in the Far Eastern Campaign. If one reads the story of the war in Burma, of General Slim's retreat through Burma, Rangoon and Mandalay across the Irrawaddy to the Indian border, it can be seen that he made a study of Japanese battle tactics. He found that their plans remained steadfastly invariable. This knowledge was used to outwit them when General Slim returned to those areas. Another factor they established was the Japanese fervour of keeping diaries of events. These observations allowed Slim to beat them at their own game: it was proven that no matter what their losses were they would always attack to a rigid plan of action.

4. Java Jives

With the inevitable fall of Sumatra, there had been new plans formulated for the aerial defence of Java. *The Histoy of No 226 Group* tells us:" . . . toward the evening of 14th February 1942 the Dutch Commander in Palembang stated that the situation was 'well in hand', that all paratroops at Pladjoe were quickly rounded up . . ." Then he said on the 15th that his troops could not hold Palembang.

On 18th February 1942 our group was finally disbanded and we became part of the new West Group Fighter Command, still under Air Commodore Vincent. Only two squadrons would now operate from Batavia, made up of groundstaff from 242 and 605 together with the pilots of 232, 258 and 488 Squadrons. Whilst we in 242 operated from Tjililitan we had a maximum of only twelve Hurricanes, 605 having only six.

From the start we were regularly strafed, at least once a day, yet our Hurricanes were never caught on the ground. Now the pilots were learning the characteristics of the Navy 'O' (Zero), they were able to take counter measures. Hitherto, like everything else out there, the Jap fighter planes were an unknown quantity. Our pilots were quickly altering the balance of losses. Tragically, they had neither the time nor the materials to bring about a crucial change — the groundstaffs never had any doubt that if everything had been equal, the final result would have been quite different. Because the back-up was non-existent the RAF were presented with an impossible task.

The Hurricanes were dispersed openly around the airfield perimeter. There was also a smaller paddock area which housed a couple of Hurricanes undergoing maintenance — this was all without any protection. Our Hurricanes were taking off, landing, refuelling, re-arming and up again, ceaselessly carrying out strikes around the clock. We were not losing many of our few aircraft at this particular time — certainly not in combat, though one or two became unserviceable.

On the 19th Taff Simmons and Sergeant Pilot John Isedale were getting John's aircraft ready for take-off. As they finished, John climbed into his cockpit and off he went accompanied by the others. No sooner had they disappeared from view than they appeared to be returning as one of the lads looked up and said:

'Bloody hell they're back — p*** off and give us a break.'

'Something must be wrong, surely' added another.

Three or four planes were approaching wing tip to wing tip as though on some celebration fly-past, prior to landing. From where we stood they looked like our own — then all hell was let loose as four A6M Zero's peeled away. Chorused voices screamed 'Christ they are bloody radials — Japs!'

The very versatile Zero could reach over 300mph with a range of some 1,000 miles and could carry 2 × 132lb bombs along with their armament of 2 × 7.7 guns and 2 × 20mm cannon. We all aimed for the lead position in our race for cover diving behind nearby packing cases — the only cover. This is one occasion on which the groundstaffs must take their share of dangers — one of many, if you were lucky.

The first bullets and shells zipped up off the grass about twenty feet ahead. Some had helmets on, something I never remember having had at any stage. My friend Taff was trying very hard to bury himself into the baked hard ground and imitate a Dutch mole without too much success. We all held the same terror of strafing and each time did nothing to reduce that fear. That raid did not develop further, though it did show how simple it was for the Japs once our aircraft had left. Eventually the four craven cowards emerged from behind their packing cases and a less amusing aspect came to light. First, I noticed Taff's elbow had started to bleed profusely, yet he was unaware that he had been nicked. Then, another fitter yelled out: 'Hey, look what you silly sods have been hiding behind.' We looked at the case contents and found to our horror that each one held six bottles of breathing oxygen, all fully charged. Oh, what fools we mortals be!

There were no more raids that day so just before dusk we were released and we slunk back to our billets. In the evening we washed and cleaned up then sat down for a card game, in no mood for gaiety.

Next day, we found some Dutch Air Force groundstaff at the drome. They had with them a couple of Brewster Buffalo's (best described as bullocks) parked near our service area. The engines had been started and run-up with no sign of any aircrew. I always said this particular aircraft was a disaster and now I was seeing further confirmation. It was short, fat and stunted like a beer barrel fitted with an engine, and when the engine started up it couldn't make up its mind whether to continue running or cough up its innards and report sick. The complete engine then became enveloped in smoke as though attempting to hide away in shame from any onlookers. The noise from its Wright-Cyclone engine when taxiing did nothing to justify its very faltering power. Further, it reminded me of an over-affectionate bulldog loath to leave its kennel. I admit this anecdote of the Buffalo is biased, yet any groundstaff who had them thrust upon them as front line aircraft would agree with those sentiments. I hated to think how any of our Buffalo pilots felt when faced with the Zero — one thing for sure, he needed to be brave!

Next day, as part of our daily schedule, we were bombed and strafed to let us know it wasn't just all a bad dream. The incoming belligerents were becoming more and more impudent, and their run-in's were more selective and made from different angles of attack. It was not always easy to find cover as they kept changing their direction of approach. Our latest casualty was a wounded Bill Hocken whose leg was hit by either shrapnel or cannon shell, and he was followed by a shocked petrol bowser driver who got one through his cab window. At least the time spent on the drome was a reminder of home during the Battle of Britain days — the rest of our days here in the Far East were more often than not an enigma.

When we arrived back that night it was to find that everyone had moved out to yet another home, a well-known barracks named Lan Trevelli. Picking up our bits and pieces we played the usual follow the leader game. Lan Trevelli housed many Dutch (white) troops, and when we arrived we found them all laid out on their beds — each with his 'Dutch wife' held between his legs. Let me hasten to add this was not a case for a mass court marshal but the use of a pillow placed between the legs to allow air to flow and reduce perspiration. Certainly our arrival did not disturb their peace or even cause a second glance in our direction. I have to say they looked spick and span, neatly dressed with creases still in place. We couldn't help but wonder how their present deployment in town was enhancing their war effort.

The days rolled on relentlessly, our working clothes becoming sweated and tattier by the day: we were able to keep ourselves washed but there was little opportunity to do more. The indigenous population were still cheering as we travelled between barracks and airfield. There was no doubt in our minds that amongst those cheering would be many almond-eyed Asiatics collecting their statistics. Despite rumours that Jap attempts to invade had been repulsed, they had not yet attempted any landings on Java. We should have known better than to listen to rumour for, after all, there had not yet been a convenient Sunday.

On Saturday afternoon, 28th February 1942, *The History of No 266 Group* tells us: ' . . . Air Commodore Vincent, with seven members of his staff, proceeded to Bandoeng. They were instructed by Air Vice Marshal Maltby to carry on through the night to Tjilijap. There they boarded the ship *Zaandan* which arrived at Fremantle on 8th March 1942. The two squadrons were left in the care of Wing Commander Maguire. Owing to wastage, only one squadron was now operating 242. The pilots of 605 were sent off to evacuate if possible. No 242 Squadron under Squadron Leader Brooker, DFC, continued to operate with conspicuous success engaging the enemy aircraft and strafing enemy forces. Heavy casualties both in personnel and aircraft were inflicted upon the Japs. On 6th March 1942 Squadron Leader Brooker was instructed by Air Vice Marshall Maltby to leave by air for Australia in a Dutch Loadstar, taking with him a number of pilots. At this stage only five serviceable Hurricanes remained. Wing Commander Maguire was instructed to leave but he apparently elected to stay with his few remaining pilots of 242 Squadron who had continued to operate magnificently right up to the very end . . .'

Evidently the Jap concentration of forces was at this moment lurking round the shores, having left Java as the last objective — probably expecting to meet stronger resistance. Our large force, by head count, included a great number of RAF personnel who were not really trained in the art of front line warfare. We believed the enemy had misread the situation and expected to be met by a 'well-trained' army force equipped to fight. It had long been thought that we had originally been intended to be a decoy — 'Churchill's gift to Nippon'. It gave a short breathing space to Australia for her to prepare for the worst, should it come to pass.

Sunday 1st March 1942.

Japanese troops came ashore at several places on the island. The squadron, now greatly depleted, was more busy than ever before, if that were possible. The four or five Hurricanes came and went in rapid succession — up and down, up and down endlessly. We could only be in awe of those young men in their cockpits. Never once did we hear a moan or complaint, except for the curses of a few battle-tired men left behind to fight it out alone — but we remember them. In fact, in our squadron, we considered them to be our Far Eastern 'few', and there is no greater compliment than that.

Mention was now being made of General Wavell's departure to Australia. If he and his party were going then things didn't look too good for us. Strangely, no one ever mentioned the impending possibility of being incarcerated — assuming that prisoners would be taken at all. Maybe that thought was why no one discussed it. However, we did think that for all his authority, the general had been handed a disastrous and hopeless situation — just as the RAF had. It now appeared that, of all the RAF forces on the island, it was only necessary for ourselves to remain. Unfortunately for the others it was too late to extricate themselves from the chaos; many tried from Tjilijap and other coastal areas but not many were successful.

The Allied naval force was by this time bedded down in Davy Jones' locker and there could be no way out without our Navy. On 25th February 1942, the cruiser *Exeter*, the destroyers *Electra, Encounter* and *Jupiter* and the Australian cruiser *Perth* sailed from Batavia to join the Eastern strike force at Sourabaya, before meeting the Japs in the Battle of the Java Sea. A mixed Allied force of Australian, British, Netherland and American ships were grouped. It consisted of eight cruisers, twelve destroyers, thirty-two submarines and a number of auxiliary craft. Against this small and inadequately equipped force, unprotected from the air, the Japanese fleet were able to employ overwhelming strength in this last stage of their conquest.

The first invading convoy was sighted on the 26th approaching from the north-east — the Allied ships sailed to engage them. In the eight-hour battle that ensued, two Dutch cruisers, *De Ruyter* and *Java*, and one Dutch and two British destroyers, *Kourtener, Electra* and *Jupiter*, were sunk. The cruiser *Exeter* was hit and returned to Sourabaya to undergo repairs, bury her dead and then attempt to reach Colombo. The Australian cruiser HMAS *Perth* and the American *Houston* sailed for Tjilijap but before they reached the Sunda Straits they met and sunk two Jap transports before being sunk themselves.

On 1st March 1942 the damaged *Exeter* was sunk. A large number of survivors were picked up by the Japs and placed in camps on Celebes (Macassar). HMS *Encounter* was sunk the same day; only four ships survived. That battle, despite the sacrifices made by all the Allied ships taking part, delayed the invading force by less than 24 hours.

How does one justify such losses in known unequal circumstances?

At Tjililitan airfield our first two days into March were hectic as we took poundings from the Japs. On Tuesday 3rd March, we climbed aboard our trucks and moved out taking the road south-east; our next stop would be the drome at Andir, near Bandoeng. Andir would be a welcome change for it was hill country where the Dutch took their rest from the heat during the hot season.

We had not travelled far before we came to a stop and for no apparent reason the convoy turned and headed back from where it had come. Just as we were about to reach the airfield we were warned of another air attack. The noisy drone of hostile aircraft almost drowned the noise of our trucks. Very deftly we removed our bodies from the vehicles making a swift and direct bee-line for the ever available irrigation ditches. At this point the Jap bombers, in their familiar number of 27, were about 15,000 feet high in a tight formation. The first cargo was dropped and came hurtling down towards us but not, thank God, on us. Had we not immediately taken cover we would have been directly under the full load — to date we had surely lost the first one or two of the proverbial nine lives.

The next day was 4th March 1942, and passing thoughts told me I had been going the 'wrong way' since France in 1940; this time it looked as if there would be no way out — I could be caught. Before the convoy moved off again for Andir, a call was made for a volunteer dispatch rider using a Royal Enfield 500cc machine. I couldn't understand why this golden opportunity was not being grabbed by older men at first:

'Here Sarge, I can ride that bike.'

'OK Corporal but can you really ride this one? It's almost as big as you,' came the wisecrack I could expect from my old friend Sergeant Peake — it was a great shame that he had only months to live thanks to the treatment yet to come. I must surely have been suffering the early symptons of a cerebal malaria when I replied:

'No problem Sarge, sure I can ride it, they are all the same.' 'Aren't they?' I asked myself.

This time the squadron was going to be better organised and I was to lead it — I was to go ahead and ensure that at all times the road ahead remained clear and safe. I was to report back by waiting for the squadron at my chosen points from time to time or report immediately any obstructions encountered or any sighting of the enemy. I should have thought twice about the latter part of those instructions. 'Sighting of the enemy.' Why didn't I think that they might sight me first? Obviously everyone else had. However, even those lucid instructions cut no ice with my dulled brain and all I could think of was getting on that bike. I had not admitted to my very limited experience, for it amounted to a mere few months on a 250cc Red Panther! It was bought for my seventeenth birthday by my father at the cost of £2.10.0 deposit and 6/3d a week until £29.0.0 was paid. Shortly afterwards I joined the RAF and did no more motor cycling. I'm sure my sergeant had not found the best qualified man for the job, but I was the only volunteer.

I had no problem starting the Royal Enfield though I did find the weight quite a handful whilst stationary. I moved off at a steady pace, determined to be careful for fear of losing the job. I was totally unaware of those saying: 'The silly young bugger'. Slowly and carefully, I left the barracks with the small map and verbal instructions. I thought there was nothing to worry about as there appeared to be only the one main road — how could I go wrong?

I last remember Taff Simmonds sitting in the front seat of a 30cwt truck, rifle resting across his knees, about to shut the door: 'Take care, Jim and leave one or two Nip's for us.' I had mounted the machine whilst still a young and naive, but normal man. My hand gripped the throttle and I let in the clutch to be born again. As the adrenalin flowed, I was transformed into Stan Woods, England's number one rider, winner of many Isle of Man trophies and holder of records. Why should I care about a few thousand Japs?

My fantasy world had opened up for me at last — right then I cared nothing about anything or anyone, least of all the enemy. Surely if these myopic creatures with their slit eyes and yellow skins saw me approaching they would scatter? With the wind howling and blowing the warm air across my face, and with a comforting touch of the revolver I had been given, one more twist of the throttle told me life was great. Straddled across the open road tearing through many *kampongs*, I scattered chickens and ducks as they waddled their way across. My style and carefree attitude, though perhaps typical of my youth, was none the less arrogant. Still I sped on towards the lessons to be learnt.

Somewhere between Batavia and Buitenzorg and still on the main road, I headed for a place named Tjitloeroeg; it was there I intended to wait for the squadron and do a check before moving on again. I stopped some distance from Buitenzorg on the Tjitloeroeg road to give my legs a stretch and wait. The miles had flown by. I waited about twenty minutes without any sign of the convoy. At first I reasoned that maybe I had travelled too fast and left the convoy further back than I realised. Alternatively they may have stopped for a break, though I could think of no suitable place along the way. Perhaps I was still in the grip of that Devil speed who had taken over my reasoning faculties, so I proceeded at a slower pace thinking that the convoy would eventually catch up with me. I looked around at the beautiful scenery; it was most difficult to imagine this lovely island was in turmoil. The road had a great high wall on my right, and on my left, a long drop into the paddy fields below. The earlier light rain had stopped and the day was now bright and sunny once more. A little worried, I told myself that as I had seen neither enemy nor obstruction, and as the convoy was following me, all must be well.

I soon convinced myself I had done no wrong and I remember so clearly how I once again 'hit speed' on the straights. Boy-o-boy was I getting good — or maybe just a little too clever. I promised myself that I would do this job again if I was required.

Approaching a bend in the distance with the same measure of irresponsibility as at all previous bends, I swung the bike into the bend and around the great high rocky wall. There, within a frighteningly short distance and directly in front of me, were two trucks spaced across the road. Never since have I experienced such a 'gut' reaction as I did in those fleeting seconds.

'The Japs are hiding in the drains. I am about to be sniped at. The convoy will be pulling up all around me and over the edge into the fields below.'

These were the thoughts that raced through my mind. If I wasn't around or alive to move the trucks or warn them, I would have failed in my task. A vital decision had to be made. Is it possible that so much can be absorbed by the average brain in such a limited time-scale which then makes your decision for you? I know it is possible.

On the right, I was faced by a confrontation with that rocky wall and its large deep irrigation ditch — the possibility of a smashed up body and bike at least. On my left I would face nothing but fresh air until I lay broken amongst the rice crop, maybe drowned. Neither way looked good and no Jap would need to bother about this intrepid dispatch rider.

I was never conscious of the decision-making going on in my brain and aimed for the drain. If I had bounced off the wall just a little less hard I would have dropped in on a near perfect two-point landing. As it was, I bounced into the drain, rear wheel first with the front one pointing to the sky, and landed on my back in the bottom of the drain. It was another piece of luck that the bike had not fallen on top of me.

Eventually, I shakily hauled myself out and onto the roadside where I lay stunned for some minutes dabbing at my bleeding parts. I truly thanked God for leaving me with nothing worse than torn clothes, cuts and bruises, to say nothing of the shock. I have no recollection of how long I sat there before some of those awful shakes wore off — probably enough time for me to have been killed a hundred times over by that imaginary sniper — but still the convoy had not reached me. Why was it all so awfully quiet?

I hurt and still couldn't lift the bike out alone; I was only an unsophisticated twenty-year-old without a clue of my whereabouts, and I was alone. Perhaps, for the first time in my life, I knew what it felt like to be afraid of the unknown. By now

I realised that no Jap had pounced on me, nor was there anything to suggest that they were in the close proximity. I wondered why the trucks had been left like that, if they were not intended as an ambush. Upon closer inspection I found they were Dutch vehicles and seemingly in good shape — definitely too good to have been left as an ambush. I wondered where the owners were.

Though I had regained much of my composure I was still somewhat confused by my situation. I heard a chattering noise from along the road but could see no one. Quickly I looked for cover but there was no place except my friendly drain. My imagination was already working overtime seeing visions of howling Japs screaming *banzai*'s and I could almost feel the sharp end of a well-used bayonet. Then, as I peered over the edge of the three-foot drain I saw a bullock cart. It was some distance away but I could make out four or five figures. I was unable to tell which race they were: they could have been harmless genuine locals going about their business or the enemy posing as them whilst infiltrating. I was inwardly scared and tense — it was like 'High Noon' in the westerns as my hand found my revolver and withdrew it. Slowly those figures and their cart moved towards me showing no signs of hostility, or even concern, until they noticed the two trucks, at which point their chattering rose to a crescendo. I recognised one or two words of Malayan and thought that if they were Japs then they were excellent deceivers, but then that was one of their greatest skills.

The next few minutes seemed like a lifetime, then, to my great relief, I realised that they had to be Indonesians who showed absolutely no sign of being armed and who were looking only for a way through the trucks. Showing myself, I called 'Brenti!' knowing it meant stop or stay.

I pointed to the bike and to my wounds now wrapped up with bits from my shirt tail, then in a mixture of Malayan and my practised gesticulations I said:

'Satu orang tida mau Siya Ingris,' followed by, 'Banya orang trima casi.'

Hopefully, I had told them I could not lift the bike by myself and that I would be thankful for more help. My linguistic talent may not have been good but neither were they dumb — so they caught on. Their faces looked quite pleasant and friendly, and together they lifted out the bike telling me to stand to one side. The bike looked badly damaged but was more dented than mechanically impaired.

The natives now seemed in no hurry to leave me and I felt better. I asked them to give me a hand to move the trucks which they would need to do anyway in order to pass with their cart. With myself at the wheel the shifting was no problem; these trucks had just been dumped in a hurry and the butterflies were sending me messages again. We pushed the trucks down the road and parked them line astern, then I removed the rotor arms, and with great joy the natives let down all the tyres.

I gave them what little money I had, and attempted to start the bike — it failed the first time and my heart sank yet again. I was glad they hadn't already gone. I was envisaging a ride on their bullock cart when, with a couple of pushes from my new-found friends, the bike roared into action. One of the natives pointed to my cuts and abrasions, some still bleeding. With good sign language and my little understanding of Malayan, he told me of a first aid post about four or five kilometres ahead. I thanked them again, 'Banya trima casi,' not knowing that within three years I may have been looking into their rifle barrels as well as those of the Japs.

I came upon the first aid post manned by two Dutch ladies. One was a nurse in the Dutch forces. In very good English I was told that I was in fact heading for the coast and the enemy: I must have made a wrong turning at a junction near Buitenzorg, where the convoy could have passed me.

One of the nurses told me as she dressed my wounds that my accident had happened at a place named Puntjak Pass, and that I was now in an area which yesterday had been evacuated by most Dutch and British troops. They did not know the exact location of the enemy who were in marauding groups in many localities and moving slowly inland. Asked if I could manage alone or did I wish to travel with them into Bandoeng, I had to refuse with grace — how could a dispatch rider finish his journey chaperoned by two women? Soon I was retracing the miles back via Puntjak Pass and past the parked trucks to Bandoeng, this time at a much more steady pace!

I was a much chastened young man when I finally arrived at the barracks in Bandoeng and, seeing the squadron transport parked up, I quietly dumped the bike then walked casually inside. I entered as though I had been there for hours. Only my scratched face and a bandaged wrist could be noticed — I could say I had fallen, if asked. No one took any notice of the lone man who had just ridden in until one voice called out:

'Nice going Jim, pity about our spot of trouble.'

I was cornered and lost for an answer, if indeed an answer was required of me.

'Yes, it was hard luck,' I replied moving on as quickly as I was able.

It wasn't until much later that I found out what had actually happened; a squadron friend told me there had been an accident involving a truck with faulty brakes, which had resulted in a fatality.

The following day started brightly enough with a more comfortable atmosphere than in Batavia. We were told to hand in our few rifles which were to be passed on to the Dutch army. Something didn't ring true; why should soldiers be without rifles at this late stage? Finding it difficult to accept, a number of us failed to obey and later we were to believe it was connected with the impending surrender. There was a small cinema nearby which would be opening that afternoon, so a small bunch of 242 caballeros sat outside on the cool marble floor of the portico and waited. The main feature film was to be *Banana Grove* starring Jimmy Cagney. He played a tough-guy manager on a plantation set in some unidentified South American Republic. The rest of the cast was a horde of babbling natives complete with the local agitator.

The leader was a typical pukka sahib with the proverbial pebble in his mouth and a steamy siren of a wife who was only interested in one brand of banana — which Cagney carried around with him! The story was a series of disasters — monsoons. rains, thunder and lightning, fire and rebellion. It all seemed a little too topical for us in our present situation and we were glad to see daylight again when it was over.

March 4th brought our fateful day nearer as we set to work on Andir airfield servicing our four aircraft to get them airborne. We were armed and had pilots who still seemed to be spoiling for a fight in spite of the ridiculous odds.

The drome was large and spacious and one could see across a wide expanse toward the mountain ranges. In one particular cleft in the range, a pass or a valley, aircraft buzzed around like tiny dots. Maybe a dogfight was taking place over an area of some importance — perhaps the Hurricanes were being harassed by Zero's as they endeavoured to strafe enemy forces.

Our quiet session was broken by a single shout of: 'Look out! They are coming this way.' 'They' could have been either our Hurricanes or their Zero's; no one could tell at that distance, but we no longer took any chances. Off we dashed to a nearby bungalow which stood empty at the airfield entrance; a few preferred the shelter of nearby pomelo trees. The planes were both ours and theirs and the first Hurricane came roaring over with a Zero on its tail. Then came another Hurricane with yet another Zero on its tail. It was a grand sight to see them zoom, climb and dive as each tried to rid himself of his encumbrance. Not a shot was fired. Then, almost without warning, all the planes broke away as though by pre-planned arrangement — there was no accounting for what had looked more like a terrific air display than an act of aggression.

When our two landed they were almost out of fuel and had no idea why they hadn't been shot at — a strongly-held view was that the Japs hoped to secure at least one Hurricane more or less intact. This, they did not achieve.

In Bandoeng my two good friends Bill Webster and young Joe Parker, both long-standing members of 242, and I agreed that we would travel together in Bill's 15cwt Bedford truck. Our bits and pieces, together with the tinned food Bill had acquired and our rifles, were stored away at the ready. It looked now as though the Japs were creeping up on us, often on cycles and from all directions.

We were instructed to head for another airfield named Tasikmalaya (Lake of Malaya), which is to the south of Garoet and near Tjiamas. It was a better place from which to reach Tjilijap on the coast where there might be a way out. The journey to Tasik' was much the same as that to Bandoeng, only this time I wasn't driving!

We reached Tasik' late on 6th March 1942 to find our three Hurricanes dispersed by their pilots. We were immediately met by a flight of Zero's that were stooging around nonchalantly with their flaps down. One or two dropped very light anti-personnel bombs.

We off-loaded and dumped our meagre belongings, found a tap to wash, then ate from our own provisions. There was a definite air of despondency affecting almost everyone on that station because we had no positive instructions. Some were even talking of being lifted out by air; such crazy talk and infantile beliefs — how on earth could thousands of men be lifted out when those able to do the lifting had already gone? Even supposing a large troop-carrying aircraft had been available, it would not have climbed a hundred feet before the nearest Zero would have picked it off.

Our own little group believed we had reached the point of no return, yet found it most difficult to accept a final ending. There was nothing to do except sit around and wait in semi darkness, whiling away our remaining hours of freedom and awaiting orders. We listened to many silly and fantastic ideas which were either wishful thinking or immature reasoning. Schemes were being mooted, argued and torn to pieces. Eventually everyone found somewhere to rest and a weary fitful sleep took over.

The next day dawned with that welcome and inevitable warming sun, to find the squadron with the last three Hurricanes on the island of Java. There was no sign of the pilots who, if they had any sense, would be looking for a way out. Their stint had been more than well done and none of them deserved to be killed in what was now a totally useless action. Our position of 'wait and see' prevailed until dusk on Saturday 7th March 1942; the following day would surely change our lives completely.

Sunday 8th March 1942.

'Oh what an inglorious day *this* Sabbath be' — it was our last day as 'free men' for more than three-and-a-half years. We were to move again without knowing our destination. Bill, Joe and I jumped into the Bedford and took our place in the convoy. We had assumed that orders were being given by some suitable person who just might know what he was about. Before we left, those last Hurricanes were destroyed by a Canadian friend, Bill Yeardye, who now lives in Hamilton, Ontario.

We travelled in convoy back towards Garoet. The roadside *kampongs* looked unchanged, undisturbed and unconcerned, and the natives looked puzzled by so much movement of vehicles. Soon we arrived at a more populated area where several roads met. Many British army personnel and military police were gathered in separate groups amid much confusion. Word filtered back to us that the Dutch had capitulated, and it had been agreed that all major towns were to be declared 'open'. It was being said that this action had been taken to save further unnecessary bloodshed. We strongly suspected that the decision considered the Dutch and their families, and not us.

In retrospect, our journey to this point appeared to be part of a pre-arranged policy connected with that surrender, as did the demand for our rifles earlier. No one had thought it worthwhile to explain some of the facts to us and the general opinion was that our commanders should have had some say in the surrender. But no, we were told in no uncertain terms that if we did not hand over all arms we would later be court-martialled.

After listening to many irate servicemen and many strong rumours, some took it into their own hands to continue their freedom. Bill, Joe and I were not ready to risk a bullet from the first 'honourable' Jap to meet us on friendly terms so we turned and headed in the opposite direction — we had food, rifles and ammunition for two or three days at least. Already a few 242 lads, led by Dick Keefe, had made for the hills anticipating this very happening; perhaps we could join them and others.

So at Garoet we split from the main group of 242 Squadron, losing contact with many good and loyal friends. Most of them we would never see or hear of again, nor would many ever see their families again. Taff Simmonds and his friends were fated to travel north to Singapore, Sumatra and Japan as prisoners, whilst Bill, Joe and I would finish up back in Tasik', but only after being rounded up like cattle.

Having discussed our present position, we now needed immediate decisions. Should we try for the coast, knowing that it was most unlikely to be of any benefit, or perhaps we should head for the safer hill country? I'm sure we already knew that sooner or later we would be flushed out and seen off if we continued in our escapade. No doubt Winston Churchill would have said:

'Fight to the last — neither civilian nor serviceman should be considered,'

but then he wasn't there, was he? And that sort of statement wasn't very helpful as was shown in Singapore.

Anyway, the decision to surrender was detested even though we could appreciate that it was the only sensible decision to take. It had been distressing for many that there had been a distinct lack of opposition to the enemy; most had not even seen an angry Jap. I grant that there were first-class fighting units such as the Blackforce under Brigadier Blackburn, who fought valiantly north-west of Batavia together with other units, including the ack-ack lads. I write only generally and of action on the ground in Java and Sumatra where even the airfields we operated from gave little or no protection to pilots or groundstaffs.

So Joe, Bill and I felt we had to make our small and probably futile gesture, to hang on to our freedom just a little longer. After a short study of the small map I had retained, Bill made our very first decision:

'We'll try for somewhere around Soekaboemi or maybe Buitenzorg in the direction of the hills.'

'Sounds OK to us,' Joe and I agreed.

After a short way it became obvious that all traffic was heading in the opposite direction.

'Bill, I think we ought to check on the map again.'

'OK, if you feel that need,' came Bill's reply.

Before long, as more and more vehicles passed going the other way, Bill slowed down and stopped one. In answer to Bill's question the driver said:

'We are instructed to go into Tasikmalaya, or one of two plantations named Wanneraja and Pamegatan, because of the surrender.'

Most were coming from the west of Java where the Japs had landed at Merak and Banten Bay. We wondered if that meant the enemy were now coming in large numbers from that direction.

'Bill, do you think the enemy are not too far away?' asked Joe.

'That driver said they will already be in Bandoeng, though not in large numbers,' replied Bill, and he sounded in a hurry to move on.

He turned the Bedford and headed back eastwards. A little while later Joe said:

'Let's stop and get things sorted out.'

Without great enthusiasm, we got the map out again and yet another parley took place. We were all conscious of our own uncertainty. We did not fancy the only alternative, otherwise I'm sure we would have turned back and settled for Tasikmalaya and self internment. We were not keen for a confrontation with a force of bloodthirsty sadists, but neither did we care to be told to sit down and sacrifice our priceless freedom, especially when there was no guarantee that we would not have a bayonet penetrate at least one of our vital statistics, anyway!

Eventually, we decided on Tjilijap and the slender chance that sea transport may be available, though rumours were very strong that the port was unserviceable. We agreed to give our escapade a couple of days whilst the enemy was still thin on the ground. We would try not to be too reckless and keep a low profile — if spotted and picked up we would claim to be going in for the first time.

We headed toward Jogjakarta, some 150 miles away. After fifty or sixty miles we saw fewer and fewer Allied forces. The continuing deathly hush was awesome; everyone seemed to have gone to ground out of sight of the invading forces. As we passed a right-hand turn which led to a dust road I spotted a *kampong* a little way into the trees. I called for Bill to slow down and back up a little, until I was able to see natives wandering about — they showed no interest in our stopping.

'What is it Jim? What have you seen?' asked Bill.

'Nothing in particular, just an idea.'

I continued after a moment's thought: 'Let's go in casually and ask for food — at the same time we can listen for words or expressions that may pass between them in the way of information.'

It was agreed that we had nothing to lose and Bill gave the final word — it seemed right that he should, for he oozed the confidence that we youngsters lacked.

Parking our truck off the road into the undergrowth, Bill lifted the bonnet to remove the rotor arm, then gave Joe and I our rifles, both to safeguard them, and to make our approach look more business-like. He then led the way about fifty yards along the path without anyone taking any notice, until we met a likely looking individual to whom I spoke:

'Mana tuan, Besar kampong — Siya mau bitchara?' was the best my linguistic talent could offer. 'Where is the headman? — I wish to speak,' is what I hoped he would understand it to say.

He replied: 'Apa bitchara?' (speak of what?).

The breakthrough had been made, so with the help of gesticulations I indicated food and said:

'Makan Siya trima casi wang OK.' (Food, I thank you, money OK).

At first he appeared reluctant to become involved and I sensed trouble — could he be a Jap sympathiser? However, when he was satisfied that we sought only food and, more important, would pay for it rather than steal it, his attitude changed and the first smile appeared. Everything went well with a few courteous bows thrown in as he motioned us towards a bamboo and *attap* hut — accommodation we would soon come to know very well. I walked ahead with the native and noticed Bill had kept Joe at the rear in case I was walking into trouble.

As you would expect, the headman was an old man with the proverbial stringy beard and pleasant face which carried more lines than King's Cross. He greeted us in a most friendly manner as the food we had asked for was being prepared. We listened carefully for the words 'Nippon' and 'Soldat'; many natives wouldn't think twice about selling us to the Japs for a few guilders, so we needed to stay on our guard.

Dusk was falling and Jogjakarta was still some distance ahead with no large towns in between. Unable to travel in the dark with any measure of safety, we decided to ask for a night's cover. If betrayed, we could give the answer that we had planned — we did not stand to lose much and it seemed a fair risk to Bill and I. Joe wasn't too keen, thinking it better that we kept to the main road and sheltered for the night in some undergrowth with less chance of being caught by surprise. Maybe he was right. However, we made further gesticulations to the headman indicating our wish to stay the night in his *kampong*. He agreed, particularly as Joe brought out a large Dutch currency note; it was rather an astute move for it was probably more than the Japs would have put on our heads. I just hoped that they would not attempt to collect both payments before morning!

The villagers were being most affable, and acting as though we were invited guests. We were probably the first white visitors they had ever accommodated. We were shown to an empty hut which didn't look too bad, all things considered, where we thankfully relaxed. Of course, we knew nothing of their other unfriendly guests who permanently resided in the bamboo — the bamboo bugs that we would come to know very, very closely. Their bite was keen and the smell disgusting — the natives must have become impervious to them over the years, as we soon would, like it or not.

Taking it in turns to stay awake, we lay on that bare bamboo and tried to sleep. Apart from the irritation and biting of our bed-mates, the night proved uneventful. At last we had been able to take in some of the native lifestyle, and we were not too keen on it! They had been courteous and honest during our short stay, so we gave them more money then went on our way.

Our plan was to continue along the same route to Jogjakarta. Bill replaced the rotor arm, checked that nothing had been disturbed then reversed out from the undergrowth. All the good and valuable advice we had been offered as youngsters about freedom could now be measured — we were finding that its true value was grossly understated as no one can estimate the true value of freedom whilst he still enjoys it. To think that your life could be lost with one swift and painful thrust of a bayonet was frightening when it was so close to becoming reality. Nevertheless, with each step we took we had to satisfy our own conscience, or ego, that forward was the only direction to go in order to maintain our freedom.

The area we now passed through was again like a morgue on a Bank Holiday — it was as though everyone had picked themselves up and walked away. We realised that the enemy would have made landings at eastern points such as Sourabaya, and that the two armies would move towards the centre where they could consolidate. For the moment we believed our position was about central on the island — probably the safest spot and the last area the enemy would reach in large numbers.

We had been given to understand that when the Japs came upon large groups in a state of surrender they were totally bemused. In their previous campaigns against China and Russia, they recognised only torture and annihilation of their enemy. Now they found themselves faced with thousands of prisoners but with no rule book. Having no idea what to do they simply left prisoners to their own devices until they gained full control of the situation. Yet if any group of prisoners at that time had made a concerted effort to hold out or take up arms, they would have been slaughtered. Also, many of the indigenous populace and all service personnel would have been sacrificed in the bloodbath of gigantic proportions.

Jogjakarta was now only ninety or so miles further east, and if the town was still free, perhaps we could join with a larger party. With that in mind on 9th March 1942, we pressed on, albeit not very confidently. We knew that if we had the opportunity of joining others and declined to do so, we would be putting ourselves at greater risk. Joe suggested that we put a deadline on our plans and Bill agreed:

'OK, we go as far as Jogja'. If nothing changes for the better then we turn and go like a bat out of hell back to Tasikmalaya.'

This was a fair and wise decision to which we readily agreed. Bill continued:

'Just hope the Japs are not already at Tasik' when we do finally arrive.'

The road was still quiet but the town was the opposite as hundreds of people thronged the streets like lost souls — both Indonesian servicemen and Dutch whites. Many were in family groups making preparations for whatever they envisaged was about to happen to their lives. Some Dutch servicemen had hurried back home after the announcement of the capitulation to be with their families — it must have been a most traumatic time for them all. There was utter chaos as nobody seemed to know where the enemy was, or even what to do in their own best interests. Now there were three more to add to that total.

Leaving Joe in the parked Bedford, Bill and I set out to seek advice. We were told that the Japs, now without opposition, were slowly garrisoning the larger towns and they saw the British and Allies as interfering in Java. It was considered that the Japs would be spiteful toward us, so our advice was to turn around and get back to Tasik' and fast.

We were given some hospitality in Dutch barracks where everything was thrown open to all-comers, then we prepared for our inevitable return into captivity. By midday we found ourselves back in the vicinity of our previous night's stay — the *kampong*. We decided on a stop and received a most hearty welcome (for us, or our money?). All was still quiet as I asked:

'Nippon mari sini?' (Nippon come here?).

'Tida Nippon mari sinni,' (No Nippon come here) replied the native.

We requested food hoping to hang on to our own few tins. The request was greeted with many smiles — they had no doubt seen the glitter of Dutch silver; with more vision and wisdom we would have held on to the money we had. We were given a plentiful serving of rice on a huge palm leaf decorated with pieces of dried fish and other tasty morsels: it was delicious. At any other time this exercise would have been a very enlightening experience. However, we needed to push on quickly, so we made payment and wished them well.

Some miles from Tasikmalaya Bill pulled to a halt. He wanted a discussion. At this point we were safe, or so it seemed, and we should decide our next move — whether to continue using the Bedford or to abandon it and take to our legs. It was not possible to judge when or if we would meet any Japs at this late stage.

'Either way,' said Bill, 'we have no option but to dispose of the ammunition and rifles — they would be a clear death sentence if found with us.'

I thought we should dump everything except our personal gear, and Joe agreed as we could then claim to have been walking for a couple of days if caught. Bill was not convinced:

'Just suppose whoever stopped us had themselves come from Tjilijap. Wouldn't they have seen us and picked us up or shot us?'

'No, not if we had been alert and gone into the undergrowth.' was Joe's reply.

Bill wasn't one for arguing and he agreed to dump everything at a bridge we had passed earlier.

The bridge he spoke of was about four or five miles further on and we found that one or two trucks had already been launched down into the gulley. We smashed the rifles against rocks and buried the two revolvers, then, removing the caps from the full cans of petrol, we threw them down into the gulley. After stripping the wiring and yanking off any leads we smashed the cylinder head the best way we could, before pushing the Bedford down. Judging by the lack of traffic activity all of Java must have been put to flight or incarcerated.

'Now tear your shirts and make yourselves look even more scruffy than you are,' was Bill's order.

I was slow to respond to the shirt tearing — I only had the one I stood up in — and Bill chastised me:

'For God's sake, don't forget you have been walking two days. Would you like to stop for a shave, too?'

William was now getting testy for no one had shaved for at least two or three days, but Joe and I got his message and looked scruffy.

Taking to the road we walked three or four miles passing only one or two natives who were also on foot and, oddly enough, they still gave their courteous bow. I find it most difficult to explain or describe how I felt at that time — somewhat bemused no doubt though I've never been sure. Not knowing what lays ahead is often much worse than whatever is in store. I know I sometimes thought of my future — if in fact I was to have one — and it was that very doubt which disturbed me the most. I was also apprehensive about our first confrontation, sensing those moments would be the most dangerous of all.

Suddenly, we heard a noise — someone was coming!

'Sit down quick, as though flogged and resting — stay by the roadside and keep your hands on show.'

Bill's quickly-given advice was, as usual, up to scratch. To our relief, a 30cwt British truck came into view. Then we saw the occupants of the cab. To my dying day I shall remember the truck screaming to a halt and the minutes that quickly followed, because the Japs never did anything in a quiet and orderly fashion. Two jumped from the front cab to be followed by four or five who leapt like rockets from the canopy-covered rear to surround us. With the most fearsome blood-curdling yells and snarls they adopted the attitude of a well-trained firing squad — ever ready for the shoot. There were no butterflies in my stomach — they had died from aggravated shock — and one way or another we seemed destined to follow suit. My only thought at the time must have been 'Good God, why do they have to try and frighten us to death?' Although scared, some inner voice told me not to show it.

The four or five who had come from the rear of the truck looked like fierce warriors from out of the seventeenth century. These Japs were not short and comical, nor were they myopic or in shabby uniforms: they were every inch soldiers — and if they were front line soldiers then we understood how they came to move so swiftly through Malaya. What seemed like five minutes passed without any one of us having bled or died — that had to be a bonus and maybe a good omen — but orders were continually screamed and presented in an aggressive manner. I now knew what real live Japs looked and sounded like face to face and it would be a long time before I cared very much for them.

We couldn't understand a word of their language but a prod here and there with a rifle barrel told us exactly what they wanted from us. They did not attempt to sadistically molest us, though they were rough and without ceremony. The *gunso* (sergeant) pulled Bill to one side and put him in the front cab, then he had us pushed headfirst over the tailboard and into the truck. I said to Joe:

'I wonder if Bill . . .' I wasn't allowed to finish.

'Kurra-Kono yaro Tida Bagoos!' (Stop stupid fool) screamed the nearest guard.

His displeasure was accompanied by a dig in the stomach which only emphasised it was not a good time to talk. Are you surprised that I never spoke another word as I quickly remembered the nasty habits they were reputed to have? I had wanted to ask Joe why he thought Bill had been selected for a front seat — obviously not as our courier on a holiday excursion! After some time it dawned on me that they had already decided who our leader was — Bill's appearance being somewhat 'warrior-like' would equate with their own reasoning. It began to look like they were a specialist pick-up party, used wherever the need arose.

Within ten minutes we had reached Tasikmalaya, entering through the same gate we had left a long three days earlier. Having achieved very little, except perhaps a minimum of self-satisfaction, we now had to face the music and that dreadful unknown quantity once again.

The camp was littered with our service vehicles, and hundreds of men wandered about like lost sheep and slept on floors of hangars, sheds and vehicles. We learned that a number of people had escaped but many had returned to sneak back in again undetected. To an outsider the situation at Tasik', and no doubt many other places on Java, would have looked rather crazy.

We were chucked off the truck as though we were rubber balls — something we would get used to. In the Jap office we stood about as the reports were wildly shouted and the echoes ricocheted around the walls. With all the yelling and the pig-like grunting which seemed to arrive from the very depths of their stomachs, we feared the worst. The office staff and guards were like some formidable puppet show without any funny men, and the guards were much rougher and more ignorant than our recent captors. Bill had been taken somewhere else but we could not ask where. He seemed fated to suffer more punishment than ourselves, maybe even interrogation by the hated and infamous *Kempetai* (Gestapo).

Some prisoners had been paraded round the streets, after being badly beaten up, for the entertainment of the locals. Joe and I received a not-so-playful slap or two across the face as we entered the office — their usual way of welcoming guests; they don't always bow and scrape! Now that the talking had finished we were helped by their footwear into a small lock-up room used as a cell. For the next few days Joe and I were guests of their Emperor and introduced to a number of their working practices when dealing with 'naughty' boys.

'Joe,' I said, 'If this is the worst we get we have much to be thankful for.'

'They haven't even warmed up yet,' was Joe's happy reminder of what might be.

On the third day, having only received automatic bashings for no apparent reason, I was 'dying', but only for the noxious weed. I was having withdrawal symptoms so when the next guard came in, I politely asked him for a cigarette:

'Aba roko trima casi.' (Have cigarette, thanks).

Now this particular guard was the only one who had refrained from having a dig at us with some form of karate chop each time he passed. Showing a half smile on his face — maybe it was sneer at my request — he replied:

'Ahso nanti nanti,' (OK wait) and off he went.

He returned with a packet in his hand and I thought 'They aren't all that bad'. He struck a match and lit the cigarette, then as he bent down I gave a good imitation of the Jap battle cry, more in surprise than actual pain. This so-called 'decent guy' had just introduced me to yet another of their little jokes by extinguishing the cigarette on my calf. That same guard turned out to be a real rotten bugger, especially when he turned around and gave me the bent and broken cigarette, knowing I possessed no matches.

This was the first time I had seen a Korean guard and that incident was mild by their standards. I never requested another cigarette, but I still became an ashtray on a number of other occasions: I carry the scars to this day! I could not protest too vehemently or it would have wound him up to continue further. Of course, we later learnt just how lucky we had been for we weren't tortured in any of their many skilful ways. Many men brought in afterwards were beaten badly and often tortured by the *Kempetai* and others were simply shot. Apart from a number of introductory 'slappings' and 'burn ups' we were left intact and released into the camp with a stern warning and a handful of bananas.

As ever my first pleasure was to search for any 242 Squadron friends or locals from my home town area. Dick Keefe and Bill Peake who had gone into the hills from Batavia had walked into camp two days after ourselves and avoided capture. Goulding, Banham and Jock Cummings plus one or two others were still together and the remainder had gone via Pamegatan into the hell hole of Boi Gloddock jail, then on to Sumatra and Japan. Others had been sunk by a Yank submarine whilst on their way to Singapore. As Joe and I walked through the camp looking for these lads, we heard the boisterous call of Jock Cummings:

'Where the hell did you pinch those bananas?'

Joe was hanging like grim death onto the large bunch of bananas the Jap guard commander had given us.

'Nippon Emperor presento,' he said, suggesting at the same time that we should now behave ourselves or suffer the fury of the great *Dai Nippon*. We had been bemused by this action — after they had behaved so badly toward us they now expected us to accept fruit and balance the score. This was the first time that I had witnessed Japanese double standards, but in those circumstances you swallowed your pride and satisfied your stomach and its need of vitamins.

Still very concerned about Bill's fate, we made enquiries through our own commandant. The Japs had said that Bill had been sent on to another camp because he had malaria — if this were true then they had injected it as he had been in great shape when he was taken away. No one believed their story, and most thought that as leader of our small party he had been handed over to the *Kempetai*. I never did find Bill, or indeed any record of him; he was greatly missed by Joe and me.

Our first combine had already been split asunder. Amongst local lads such as Reece Richards, Ron Taylor, Pat McGrogan and 'Boy' Jelly, was my best friend, Ted Chester, who would take Bill's place and remain a lifelong friend. With our remaining money, Joe, Ted and I were able to trade a little with the natives who lined the perimeter with their baskets of Eastern foods. As far as I can remember there were no working parties; we just sat around and talked and worried, with some playing cards or the odd game of football. The place and its meaning was truly a non-event, though it was a useful time to weigh up potential friends and to form combines. Each combine contained three or four lads with a genuine wish to help one another through the testing times which lay ahead. One day a Jap commandant, stood up on a dais to give us a pep talk which finished like this:

'The Australians are my friends.

The Dutch are my slaves.

The British are my enemies.'

He seemed perplexed to hear a ripple of cheers, for he did not understand the compliment he had bestowed on us. Incidentally, in the very early days the Japs attempted to sway the Australians by showing small favours — that was to quickly change!

It was here at Tasik' where I met another Bill — a 'local' from Cumbria. This Bill made it home for a short time before finally migrating. 'Copperplate', as he was nicknamed, had arrived at Tasik' from Singapore Island after a spell in Malaya and this is how he remembers Singapore just before it fell.

Messages and rumours were flying around Singapore Island when Bill arrived including one believed to have come from the War Office. It was claimed that Winston Churchill had issued a directive that no one should be spared, neither civilian nor serviceman.

On the night of Friday, 30th January 1942, all British forces retreated from Malaya by way of the Causeway — some 30,000 troops led by the Pipers. The Argyle and Sutherland Highlanders had fought valiantly all the way from Siam with their Pipers always in close attendance. The civilian populace and most of the servicemen in Singapore were not aware of that final retreat to the island and it was not until the next morning that most of the people in Singapore realised the island was under siege.

On Sunday, 8th February 1942, the Japs attacked Singapore across a wide front around the north-west coastal areas. They were using their crack division, which I understand was known as the Chrysanthemum division. During an incursion, the Alexander hospital was attacked by a marauding party of bloodthirsty Japs. When they were first seen by hospital staff a white flag of truce was shown, as the hospital was crowded with the sick and wounded. That same flag of truce was totally ignored and met by screams of *banzai* as the Japs at once took the life of the flag bearer. Soon afterwards they entered the hospital with bayonets fixed, like the wildest of carnivorous animals, and they purposely ignored the pleas of the staff for the lives of the ill and dying who were unarmed — something the Japs could never understand.

Those barbarians systematically crushed heads with rifle butts, and with obvious pleasure thrust their bayonets into the throats and stomachs of bed-ridden patients. Some men awaiting surgery had to watch the blood gushing and spurting from others before their own turn came, and even the surgeons were given the same treatment.

Those particular Japs made that frenzied attack in an inhuman manner on helpless unarmed people. The carnage they left behind them could only be matched by similar behaviour wherever they fought. Only one or two people, who had hidden in cupboards or fled, had survived that bloodbath. I leave it to readers to judge if one *should* forget such happenings, even if it were possible to do so.

Sunday 15th February saw the fall of Singapore. Soon after dawn on the 16th, the Japs entered Singapore in force as the victors. In just seventy days they had advanced over six hundred miles from Singora in Siam to Singapore, averaging nine miles a day through supposedly impossible jungle. The general consensus of opinion in POW camps was that the politicians and the War Cabinet of that day did not heed the ample warnings of the Military. They then permitted the generals to shoulder the blame — has anything changed?

Copperplate Bill had seen many civilians commissioned into the forces just prior to the surrender. This created much consternation and dissension amongst the other ranks, in particular the Senior NCO's. Though there were decent and useful people amongst them, none had any idea of man-management amongst their own kind. The rank and file naturally did not enjoy the leadership of those using rank as a protective shield, especially when 'true' officer material was going to be well and truly tested during their internment.

In Tasikmalaya, our lives were changing rapidly; we now lacked our freedom and found life somewhat unlike anything we had ever known or could have envisaged. The large majority of men had been used to being well-fed, well-housed and were generally of middle-class families or good, solid working class. Many, during their early service life, had become used to good food and clean facilities, usually being housed in solid brick buildings with modern and sound sanitation. Almost overnight, they found themselves thrown into bamboo and *attap* (palm leaf) 'coolie' huts with few facilities.

We started off in a stable over-populated with vermin — with bugs as large as ladybirds all enjoying our body — and we suffered the ripe smells of dirty stables. Consider, just for a moment, the traumatic changes that have to take place in the thinking and adjustment of a normal man's mind in these circumstances which we were compelled to accept. Most did adjust with very little serious grumbling or too much self pity but it seemed that patriotism didn't always come easy. It was truly amazing the adversities that one can endure when put to the absolute test, and after all, what would life be like without challenge? Certainly fear would enter the picture many times but is that not the real source of challenge?

It was about 8th April 1942 when we were told we were to be moved in a sizeable party to another camp. This created a sense of great uncertainty, which lead to an unbelievable state of tension. At times like this belief in ourselves, and of any future, was put to the test. Our captors were still very much an unknown quantity with a history of cruelty and disrespect for human life. Could we always accept whatever fate had in store or would we often be fearful of every move which we did not understand? I believe the 'acceptors' were most fortunate, because our lives did indeed rapidly become a series of unknown quantities.

So the convoy of prisoners left for the unknown and it was only when I realised we were travelling south-east that I felt the tension ease within me: at least we weren't travelling north which would surely have meant Batavia and a dreaded sea journey. Standing in an open truck, shoulder to shoulder, we experienced our first taste of Japanese sardine packing. With guards leaning against the cab, the journey became our first introduction to yet another discomfort: I cannot remember ever being allowed to crouch or in any way take the weight from my legs, and we could only obey the calls of nature as and when they decided to stop or change over their position after relieving themselves. A request at any other time was met by a grunt, snarl and often a karate chop to help us along. We were told to relieve ourselves over the sides as the truck sped along but that was never easy at the faster speeds and was certainly never appreciated by those prisoners downwind! At night, any empty space that could be found for us was good enough and we would be literally dumped — usually in dirty abandoned native buildings.

Finally we arrived at our destination, the town of Mallang, having travelled about 550 miles standing up — we were all knackered! Mallang is about 100 miles from the Eastern port of Sourabaya and when that was known to our 'clever' boys, they immediately had us embarking on a trip to Borneo or New Guinea. This time they may have got it right — not the nicest of thoughts.

It was now about 12th April 1942. We knew that Mallang had previously stationed a number of American Liberators on its aerodrome, and before they had left, they had made a right old mess of the airfield and its strip; it was rather unfortunate that we had to correct their act of vandalism.

We were taken to a brick building that was almost totally wrecked; it was our new home. With the usual fast breaking of ranks, like hounds to the hare we raced for the best spot to bed down, maybe under the kitchen sink or under a staircase . . . anywhere that gave just a minimum of cover from the rains. Our task, stated to us with pleasure, was to clear up the mess their hated enemy had left behind.

There were about six hundred other RAF people there when we arrived, and I was fortunate to find a few more 242 Squadron lads. Bill Yeardye, Don Rice and Joe Slater all finished up around Nagasaki near the second atomic bomb.

Rolling full oil drums from storage in secondary jungle to load onto rail wagons a long distance away, was my first task. The dumps were in wet and swamplike conditions and it was no picnic as the drums were dirty with a mixture of soil, oil and insects plastered around the outsides. As we trundled them along a cinder path by the sidings, the cinders became embedded into the drums. To manhandle those drums under violence and harassment, with handfuls of greasy sharp chippings digging into our as yet soft flesh, was both tiring and trying. Men were injured and slapped around for being careless when unable to prevent a drum from slipping from the rail car. Backs began to ache, hands became blistered and painful and our morale took its first real beating for we were not yet hardened to our new lifestyle. If we put a foot upon a drum to help it along, we would be accused of ill-treating the Emperor's possessions and more often than not receive a kick on the guilty leg. At first Joe and I had a few laughs at the antics of the guards, then all too soon it was to become much less funny.

At about this time men again started to talk of breaking camp. This would have been both rash and selfish, for the natives were now rather friendly toward their so-called liberators. However, there were some people in Mallang who were much better equipped than us for escape attempts and there were those who were fluent in the Dutch and Malayan languages, and who had a wide knowledge of the island, its indigenous populace and their habits. In addition, they probably had a few white contacts still outside, who may be prepared to help.

One day in June when arriving back from our working party, we were told of an attempted escape made by four RAF men. Two were ex-planters, one a sergeant pilot from Manchester and the fourth was a Malayan warrant officer of the Singapore Training Corps (STC). They had gone the previous night without being missed until they were picked up. Their chances had been relatively good as only the sergeant pilot had not lived in the East, one man was coloured and between them they had ample funds. They had reigned two nights.

Apparently the original plan had been a mass escape which included my Canadian friend, Bill Yeardye. Later it was decided a smaller party would be more suitable for the initial attempt, as the four would be 'testing the water'. If they could have quickly found a friendly *kampong* or contacts, it was just possible they may have succeeded. But now what?

We were kept on parade at *Tenko* and the four men were paraded before us; it seemed that the natives had preferred their rewards to risking their skins by helping escapees. The four were given an unholy beating, then tied up and taken to the guardroom. They were already in a sorry state having obviously been 'helped' along the way from the moment they were caught: every available boot would have been put in with great relish. On such occasions the guards quickly lined up to work themselves into a frenzy until they lost whatever reasoning they migh have possessed.

Later, the four were placed in a bamboo cage like wild animals, with no regard to even the most fundamental rules of warfare. Each night we were assembled on *Tenko* to witness them receive yet another beating before being returned to their cage. About a week later, in the middle of this disgusting display of cruel sadism, a lorryload of soldiers with machine guns entered the arena. They dispersed their machine guns with an expert efficiency to sourround us all — those butterflies were back and flapping around in my stomach. Our first thought was that there was going to be a mass annihilation for which we were not in any way prepared. I know of at least two that prayed — I'm sure there were many more — and I was maturing very quickly.

The camp commandant and his interpreter made their appearance on the scene in grand style as though playing some role in *Shogun* — they were dressed as though to attend their noble Emperor. The commandant told us that for every man who attempted to escape, at least ten others would die. Was he now to pick the 'chosen' forty to die along with the four he now held as an example? Was that why they needed to surround us with a battery of machine guns in case there was a reaction from ourselves? The answer was not long in coming and it was devastating. The four escapees were already lined up as though for execution and the guard in charge was attempting to blindfold the first. He was the Manchester-born Sergeant Pilot Eddie P*****, and he was refusing to be blindfolded. Two others accepted rather quietly and the fourth broke down to plead. I have many times hoped that in those last dreadful moments that Eddie suffered, he realised how proud we all were of him — we no doubt wondered if we could show the same raw courage. He typified the real heroes of war, unlike the vanity-decked chest of meaningless medals that is seen many times.

Whilst this was taking place the ranks began to sway to and fro as though to break. I doubt if anyone had considered ever being in such a hopeless situation. An order rumbled through and along the ranks, 'Hold it and don't be stupid.' It was very good advice. No doubt our captors would have welcomed some trigger practice on hot-headed prisoners.

Standing there together the four escapees were shot and a Jap officer followed through with his revolver to put a bullet into each. The whole affair had been carried out with great aplomb — the four now had the respect of their enemy as they were dead. We now understood a little more about our captors. It was said that the prisoners had earlier been forced to dig their own graves. The firing squad had turned out in beautiful white uniforms and were drilled with a trained respect for those they intended to kill. The four were buried and a small cross was placed at the head of each. In the eyes of the Japs the four were now dead but also honourable! It was rumoured two or three days later that two more men were shot and buried during a ceremony of their own — the two guards who had been held responsible were now also 'honourable'.

The Javanese people now seemed quite happy in the company of the Japs as they had been soaking up the propaganda since the campaign ended. Told it was 'Asia for the Asiatics', some would soon find out that their liberators only paid lip service to the real meaning of honour.

In early August 1942, we were once more on the move, this time to Sourabaya, a hundred miles to the east. It looked as though our 'clever boys' had got it right at long last and it was our turn to start losing more sleep, with worry. There was a very real dread of the seas. We hated those unfriendly submarines that lurked outside, hunting for easy prey — they haunted us.

The new camp we reached was Jaarmarkt in Sourabaya, the main Eastern port. It was already grossly overcrowded leaving us in little doubt that it was indeed a transit camp of sorts, and at once the rumours began; always the worst that man could concoct.

'This is a transit camp.'

'Yes, we are going to some island to the east.'

'It's Celebes we are bound for.'

Almost anyone could have been right for there are hundreds of islands dotted around the archipelago to the east.

There was a wide variety of nationalities in Jaarmarkt but the majority were Dutch. The latter appeared to have brought all their worldly goods with them into internment, down to their camp beds and personal bedding. Naturally, as first-comers, they had taken over all the worthwhile facilities which led to our sour grapes.

There must have been about 4,000 Dutch and 1,000 British in the camp, plus a few Americans from an ack-ack battery. Most of the British were naval ratings from HMS *Electra* and HMS *Jupiter*, the remainder being a small number of RAF lads. The buildings were all occupied so we had to settle for the concrete and stone floors mostly out in the open. The internal running of the camp was in Dutch hands and the American opinion was that it was very inefficient and somewhat corrupt. Claims of that kind were levelled at all nationalities at one time or another. The food itself was not too bad, though unfairly distributed and prepared with a total indifference and incompetence — all men, whatever nationality, who worked in a cookhouse were usually extraordinarily fat. On several occasions the Dutch native troops (Ambonese) rioted in the mess lines because of discrimination by the white Dutch against them. Washing facilities were totally inadequate and the whole camp was filthy. There was also considerable friction between nationalities and between services within the nationalities. All in all, Jaarmarkt was not the best of places from which to judge mankind — morale there was the worst I had ever seen and there was little spirit of mutual co-operation or of a united front against the common enemy.

The guard changed every hour and, in doing so, marched through the centre of the camp. Prisoners were commanded to bow with the head at waist level immediately any guard was within twenty-five yards, and to hold it until they were well past. Every man was ordered to shout 'Keirei' (salute) as loudly as possible upon sighting a Jap soldier or Korean guard. Anyone not complying with these rules, even if he didn't hear or see the action, was in trouble. Such a display of insubordination was usually answered with a rifle butt or the boot and would possibly end up in a 'slapping'.

We hadn't been in Jaarmarkt very long, maybe two or three weeks, when we moved yet again. About 2,500 men of different nationalities, plus a few civilians, were transferred to the HBS school. The Dutch remained behind. At HBS the facilities were a little better but, with no cover available, we took our rest on the cold tiled floors of verandahs.

Men were now beginning to feel true hunger as the vendors were slowly being removed from camp fences. Outside working parties were being fiercely restricted as the screws were turned ever more tightly. This was the first stage of a well-planned exercise in working prisoners to their death on a starvation diet. Not more than twelve prisoners died in HBS school to the best of my recollection but sickness began to prevail.

Strangely, I could never remember being given food during the first half of the day at HBS school. I know that we received only rice and sweet tea at midday and during the evening. It was here that we had our first bit of *Tenko* fun. Not many of the Koreans could count very well, certainly not efficiently, and time after time they could not arrive at the correct totals. Finally they decided to save time and use an abacus — the answer to all their problems they thought — yet still they could not agree with each other. It was comical, and sometimes they would even bring out a table as though expecting a long job. I really believe they were scared stiff of losing someone and having to suffer the consequences from the harsh and 'superior' Japanese officers.

During September and October 1942, other British prisoners had been in the Lyceum camp. It was from there that all officers and NCO's were moved to Darmo, a hutted camp outside Sourabaya. This left all other ranks alone in Lyceum, where remarkable, though I like to think typically British, action took place. Those 'other ranks' democratically voted and adopted new leaders and established their code of practice. This code, which primarily dealt with discipline, was properly followed — I doubt if any other race would show such pragmatism. A friend telling me of his stay in Lyceum camp remembered the following incident above all others.

Two natives were cruelly and unceremoniously dragged into the camp by members of the *Kempetai*. Each night when working parties came back to camp, *Tenko* was called and the two unfortunates were beaten in front of everyone; not a 'slapping' but a real beating with whatever instrument came to a guard's hand. Daily, often at each change of guard, they were subjected to subtle and crude brutalities. Then, not satisfied with those, the guards would carry out a number of personal indignities.

Over a period of some five or six weeks, not one day remained free of some form of punishment — only occasionally were the natives molested less than twice each day. I have no idea what their crime was supposed to be, except that they refused to be subdued. The two showed such remarkable courage, and were never once seen to cower or plead. Their bravery was such that one wondered just why they were being so harshly treated, even allowing for the inherent cruel streak of their captors. Many believed they were not the usual run-of-the-mill native, and daily the lads' admiration grew for them.

Means were sought to help, if only to give some encouragement. Unfortunately this was never possible as the guardroom looked directly onto the tree to which the two were tied when outside. On three sides of the quadrangle were verandahs where our lads slept — they could hear the pain suffered by the two as they attempted to move their injured limbs. On a number of nights the lads were awakened by guards who had come especially to inflict more pain on their helpless adversaries. It was like being awakened from a dream only to find it was reality. In our weaker moments we began to wonder if the Korean guards should be pitied a little, and less hated, considering they were under the heel of Jap masters. They had been conscripted into a Jap army which had a terribly harsh military code and were then considered almost as scum with no rights. Now, in us the prisoners, they had found another group of men and women upon whom they could serve similar treatment and humiliation — it was at least understandable.

January 1943 found us back in the Jaarmarkt camp having returned from the HBS school. Not a great deal of outside work was being done, except by those who opted to work in a string factory — one of the few jobs that gave a token payment of a few cents. The few cents were most helpful in buying a little extra food when able to find a discreetly-placed native.

It was in Jaarmarkt that we were given another pep talk by a member of the Jap hierarchy who ended his chat:

'You will be safe in my hands.'

Yes, those fellows were great jokers, and as deceitful as ever, for he then placed in charge of us the most fearsome, unpredictable and bullying *gunso*, who we soon appropriately named 'Blood'. Before we left for our cruise on the *Amagi Maru* another friendly *gunso* whom we knew as 'The Bull', broke one of our officer's arms — just in time for him to enjoy his cruising holiday!

So ended March 1943. Behind us were many experiences which we had never expected nor wanted. It is, however, a salutary thought that the past year may have prepared many of us for the worst which was yet to come!

'Remember that the spirit of life is endurance!'

5. To Hell and Maybe Back

THE COMBINE

The Japanese prisoner of war scene as I saw it was a melting pot of humanity.

It made a man or it broke him.

If you survived, it was with a different set of values to most other men.

You found that you were taking out of life only that which you put in.

Life became only a matter of survival — not selfish survival for no man could go it alone.

Even the strongest would at times be helpless in the steady grip of disease. Sometimes only the ministering of another man kept you alive.

When you were down you needed a friend.

When you were up you gave back what you could.

We came through knowing much more of true values and isn't that what really should matter in life?

Bill ('Copperplate')
1984

At the beginning of April 1943, rumour had it that a large-scale movement of prisoners was imminent, and for once the rumour was correct. *Tenko* was called and attended by a Japanese Doctor who was flanked on either side by his orderlies and guards — it appeared that a medical inspection was about to take place and no doubt it would reach the usual standard of a walk past.

'Strip off!' came the order from Kasiyama (the interpreter).

My stripping off did not take too long; I only possessed the shirt and shorts I stood in and many others didn't even have a shirt — the bulk of clothing had by this time been bartered for essential food.

If the *Guiness Book of Records* ever included the 'fastest medical', this one would have won hands down. In single file, showing the Doctor only our side view, we walked past his table at normal pace. 'Ugh', 'Grunt', 'Snarl', 'OK ga' and 'Lecas' (hurry) were just five of the noises he made that we understood. One quickly gained the impression that he was not too enthused with his labours, but then neither were we. Only those who could show blood were pushed to one side; many others were suffering ills much worse than a bloody wound which any doctor worth his salt could readily see, but he was just another tool of his all powerful Military. All he intended to recognise as genuine incapacity was blood and we soon learnt that no matter the cause of your blood-letting, the very sight of it might save your face and get you excused.

All those able to walk in a straight line were passed fit, and even then they allowed a foot or two either side of the imaginary line. Then came the final indignity.

'Alle men bendo!' came the cry in halting English.

Then along came an orderly with a box of glass slides and one of these was inserted into each rectum then returned to another box — we had just taken part in a test for dysentery. No one had any recollection of anyone noting which slide belonged to whom, and anyway, the next day we would be on the high seas irrespective of results. Such was the mentality, or most likely indifference, of our captors. Many had already shown very positive signs and symptoms of dysentery as well as other equally distressing and serious illness's. In short, the inspection had merely been an exercise in humiliation to weed out those who may prove to be an immediate encumbrance whilst at sea.

The next day we were called to *Tenko* for a so-called kitting out; a small amount of Dutch army greens were to be issued until they ran out, together with a shirt or shorts, maybe both if you were in the right place at the right time or if a pal was in charge. After the clothing came the Jap-style rubber boots. Like mitts, they had only one toe space for the big toe, and only two sizes were available — small and smaller. Those who could grab quickly enough took either size and if they didn't fit they would be bartered at the first safe opportunity. Those who missed the first grab, or who maybe had a pair of decent footwear and declined to take advantage of the offer, were in trouble. A prisoner having the temerity to refuse the Jap gift, even though there were not enough to go around, was insulting their Emperor. Guards at once set about those who had not collected. For their heinous crime, many were slapped around and when our CO intervened he was included in the beatings for good measure.

Next, all men were instructed to hand over any bulky possessions — these items were not just 'possessions' but were almost our last lifeline: a waterproof groundsheet, a mosquito net, a blanket or a haversack — all would prove to be invaluable. The possessions were gathered up by the guards, placed in a heap on the ground, and left overnight for heavy rains to soak the lot. Being unable to dry many things in time the next morning, much of the gear had to be left behind by order.

The night before we left, each traveller on this Eastern cruise was issued with a food ration to take on board — a half kilogram of unwashed and uncooked rice for each man, who was told:

'Take care of your food, there will be no more today.'

The same night, our last in camp, meant the Japs had their own last night out on the razzle. The infamous *Gunso* Mori (Blood), who would be running our lives from now on, demonstrated his unpleasant disposition. Returning from his night on the *attap* (tiles) boozed up, along with what seemed the rest of the Jap army, he shouted and screamed the night through — luckily without any fisticuffs. Reading between the lines, it seemed that they were non too happy with this posting and it didn't look too good for us either.

Morning dawned before many of the Japs had any sleep, so the mood was not a pleasant one as we paraded in readiness for the mystery trip. Bets amongst the lads placed us somewhere between Tokyo and Timor, so someone had to win! Whilst still on parade, we had our first incident of the day when an elderly Dutchman who had been passed as fit yet needed a stick to help him walk, raised the stick in the direction of a guard. The old chap was obviously demonstrating his disability and could so easily have been ignored, but no guard missed such an opportunity to make further trouble. The guard decided to believe the man was threatening him and now, unless he took action, he would 'lose face'. Unfortunately, worse was to follow in the bulky gorilla-like shape of *Gunso* Mori carrying his thick head of the night before; he decided *he* would handle this little matter of the old man's insolence.

It was now clear that the old chap was not only unfit, but perhaps a little unbalanced or grief-stricken. With total indifference to this, Blood beat the man about the head then kicked him in the stomach until the old boy was taken away in a very distressed condition. He missed our mystery trip so maybe he survived and was grateful for that beating — I like to think so. We had knowingly witnessed a mere foretaste of our new lifestyle. Again our CO, Squadron Leader Pitts, fully aware of the risk, stepped forward, and sure enough he too was bashed for interfering — he would have plenty more to follow that one, too.

We left the camp, many full of apprehension; those who were not, were either very brave or simply fools. We kept reminding ourselves that our 'friends' would be out there doing all in their power to put us in Davy Jones' locker. If they were looking for easy prey, then it didn't come easier than our old 3,000-ton freighter. To be trapped like sardines in their tin box would be to experience the same fate as my friends on an earlier ship — it was a frightening and horrific thought. Also, to aid submarines, the Australian Air Force would be looking for anything that moved in this area — I wanted to go home!

Eventually we arrived at the docks of Tandjoeng Perak to find our splendid ships at anchor waiting to take us God knows where. We were lined up along the dockside to be sprayed like weeds; the treatment amused us until the pungent smell hung around too long. It was so puerile though as the ship was already filthy and inhabited by all kinds of vermin.

The five or six ships were certainly not of *Cunard* standard. One of the ships was being loaded with native coolies going into slave labour — so much for their new-found freedom within that great 'New Asian Prosperity Sphere'! It seemed the Japs did not include the peasants in this promise. In this case, however, the natives need not have been too concerned, as fate was to see they didn't go very far.

As we stood at the dockside Ted asked me what I had managed to hang on to. I knew only too well what he was talking about — 'things' were what concerned Ted.

'I have a cheap watch, lighter, signet ring, my old faithful RAF housewife, a small blanket and this spoon. Those are my worldly goods.'

Ted responded: 'Eh that's not bad, between us we should be OK to do some trading with the natives.'

'I lost most of my kit back in Garoet when I was cut off from many of 242 Squadron,' I added. 'And what's more, I scrounged some of the things I have now from my friends.'

Ted then turned to Bill Pollock, the Thornaby lad who had joined our combine recently to make us four in number, and asked him what his position was. Skinny Billy, as we affectionately called him, replied: 'A fountain pen, wallet with not much in, my ring and watch. That's all I've got of any value.'

Ted continued his appraisal of our goods and chattels and concluded that we were off to a fair start, and so had to ensure that everything was kept safe and not lost in one fell swoop. Good old Ted was always the sensible organiser.

We then agreed that our combine should be finally contracted to be all for one and one for all. Joe was included in this but had not been asked what he possessed as Ted had not wished to embarrass Joe for having nothing at all. Ted and I both knew his belongings had been stolen whilst in Jaarmarkt camp because he had carelessly left his haversack lying about. He really missed the photos he had lost of his mum and dad, for he was a home-loving lad who cared a great deal. The four of us then promised each other that, unless the circumstances were exceptional, we would never dispose of anything valuable without first having a majority decision.

The *Amagi Maru* was our cruise ship, and, as far as we were concerned, was the important one. The *Matsukawa Maru* appeared to be taking many Dutch servicemen on board. The *Kunitama Maru* was yet another of the five or six ships and the *Mayahashi Maru* and the *Nishi Maru* were boarded by the 1,000 British recently arrived in Sourabaya from Batavia. Major Gibson of the 3rd Hussars was in charge of them and I understand from some ex-Hussars that the Major was well thought of as an officer. I have never been certain whether there was actually a sixth ship. If there was it may well have been the one which blew up.

Judging by the appearance of that grand fleet, we were not considered VIP's. *Gunso* Mori had by now promised us that we were going to a small island which would become our rest home. He certainly did his best to ensure his promise came true for the many who still 'rest' there. None of our party could ever understand that gentleman of very doubtful birth, but he would find his own 'rest home' not so long after those he sent so early.

'Kiotsuke!' came the order.

We pulled ourselves up to some semblance of 'attention', ready to be herded like cattle aboard the *Amagi Maru*. The first sight of the deck of this ship suggested the disinfectant should have been flooded throughout the ship rather than over ourselves. However, we had seen dirty ships before and not all were Japanese. As far as I can ascertain or remember, both the *Amagi Maru* and the *Matsukawa Maru*, had prisoners in both the fore and aft holds. These two ships were under the command of Squadron Leader Pitts for our own disciplines, and the total number of prisoners on the two vessels was 2,061. The *Kunitama Maru* had only Dutch servicemen on board — about 1,025 men in all — who were under Officer Erkelens.

The 'Grand Fleet' stayed at anchor in Tandjoeng Perak harbour from late afternoon on 15th April 1943, until the 20th. Six days rolling around on the tides is not a pleasant introduction to a sea journey in a dark and filthy hold, hungry and with your knees tucked into your chin. Those days at anchor gave us too much time to dwell on what lay ahead, and some soon began to brood on their misfortunes.

We had climbed aboard expecting it to be like any other small trooper — not luxurious but at least acceptable. That was until we saw the berth the men in front were disappearing into. We all wondered how on earth they were going to get us all into that one hold. Those at the back of the queue would probably have to park on deck which would be preferable to the depths of the hold, so we aimed to be those people, even though it could be bloody cold at night and red hot during the day.

The guards urged us on as more and more disappeared into the same hole. Helped with a push and a prod from rifle or bayonet, we were suddenly there staring into the hatch opening. The nearest guard shouted and screamed something which definitely did not mean, 'Welcome aboard Jim:

'Kurra. Baka Yaro. Dame dame Ingris.'

It actually sounded as though he was becoming a little impatient as he continued forcing more and more men on top of those still standing at the foot of the iron ladder. Inside the hold, those just entering could not move away from the ladder because of the congestion, and men began to fall over each other as they piled up trying to find space to sit down. The Japanese, it seemed, had no swear words as such but they had no bother vehemently expressing their opinion of our stupidity.

'Bloody hell, there must be over 200 already in the hold,' I thought, and the next minute a mixture of Malayan and Japanese expletives hit my eardrums.

'Kono Yaro!', 'Piggi lecas!', 'Ingris tida bagus!'

With a rough push I was half down the hole and wishing I had never joined up. I have no doubt I've been called an idiot before but never with the same venom the guard had applied. It was not the vernacular he used which upset me, but the nasty sharp prod from his bayonet and my method of entry into the 'black hole'. The same persuasion continued until the last man was parked in that one filthy cargo hold. I stood transfixed at the bottom of the steps, until I became more accustomed to the dark. I would admit to being somewhat confused and most unhappy with my lot — the place was bedlam, with everyone shouting at and cursing each other; not the curses I had come to learn and accept but the remarkable vocabulary of some long-serving servicemen. It seemed that my education was about to begin.

Only now was the full realisation coming home of the journey that lay ahead. Questions such as 'How do I get to the *benjo*? (toilet)' and 'where do we get water for the sick?' were rife and some eternal pessimists even predicted that such questions were futile as: 'They might just take us out into deeper water and pull the plug out to sink this bloody tin can.' — the fear of being torpedoed lived with us permanently. The noisy chaos continued until in good old British fashion everyone had said his piece.

Then from out of the chaos came some order. The only light hung from the hatch opening, leaving a great deal of the hold in semi-darkness. As our eyes adjusted we saw that there was not enough room to sit down in a conventional manner: we had to sit in a crouched position with our knees tucked into and under our chins. Our immediate worry was how long we could travel in this cramped situation without the all-important facilities for dealing with sickness. Survival for us meant only to live or die — there was no half-way house. Yet we would learn that this was not even a stiff test.

When everyone was in, we started to sort ourselves out. The first 'passengers' had found there were two wooden shelves around the sides of the hold, so including the floor there were three levels; this was the reason our captors had been able to push so many in when we were sure it was impossible. The Japs transported their own troops in a similar manner, including camp women, though not, of course, with the same measure of overcrowding — they always left themselves a centre floor space and enough room to walk about in.

The shelves were approximately three foot six apart and they extended five foot six towards the centre of the hold. These measurements, whilst reasonable for most Japs, were totally inadequate for the many tall Dutch and British men. There was only enough room in the centre to handle a bucket and allow a Doctor to attend one person at a time. Conditions, to say the least, were appalling, and when the first dysentery cases occurred, we realised there was no isolation space: we had no other option than to live with it, amongst the smell and filth.

We thought that coming on board last and being close to the hatch would have its compensations, as we would have more chance of escaping from a sinking ship, and would have easier access to the deck and the *benjo*'s. We soon realised that everyone else had to obey the call of nature, too, which meant they walked over us.

There was a bucket which was passed down for urination purposes, otherwise a couple of wooden box arrangements hung over the side of the ship were our toilets. There was no way a serious case of dysentery could reach such places, certainly not without assistance. The time it would take a sick man to get from his space to the toilet and back would always be too great.

Before very long *Dai Nippon* showed his ugly, sneering face, nicely framed in the hatch opening, and told us to be quiet. He echoed the usual intimidatory threats that he would close the hatch and stop the water we didn't even have. Those who were in poor shape rapidly showed every sign of dehydration and began to despair. Many had struggled along in poor health for over a year and this would probably be their final test. We had no alternative but to quieten down and make less threatening noises, for Tojo never made false threats. Friends quietly chatted, making plans to prepare for the voyage ahead and it was at this stage that many small combines were formed. Having good and trusted friends around was not only pleasant but most essential; a good friend was an insurance for life, until death finally parted you both.

It was not long before someone took charge of this motley gathering. Since our early days of captivity I had never ceased to be surprised by the stoicism shown by the average person when the chips were really down. The worse the situation became the more likely they were to rise above it if they had a true friend. Eventually, a little more space was found in the centre of the hold, as those who had held back a small space eased further in. A small area was now available for the dispensation of our rice and tea. A couple of five-gallon tins of water were sent down to us, together with an old tin as a measure, and orders were given to use it sparingly — how else could we issue it to 250 very thirsty people, many dehydrating?

We were told that use of the toilets was only by request and the kind permission of the hatch guard. Having successfully negotiated his way through all the bodies, Tommy Orton, a real Brummie character, had a nasty experience. He approached the hatch guard and said,

'Benjo ka.' (I go to toilet.)

With the usual snarl and traditional grunt the guard replied 'OK ga piggi lecas.' (OK go fast.)

Once on deck, Tommy was all eyes, taking in the seascape to see if anything had changed since we boarded. He located the toilet hanging over the side — but it wasn't the sharks trying to reach Tom's backside that caused him to shoot from his perch before he was ready. He had been looking closely in the direction of the other ships when there was a terrific explosion and one of the ships was lifted high into the air, as if still intact, only to fall in many pieces. Not knowing which ship it was, his first concern was for any prisoners that may have been on it, for none would have survived that explosion. His second thought was to get back into the comparative safety of the hold, knowing from past experience that any prisoner was fair game when something went wrong.

Inside the hold we had heard the explosion and thought it was a bombing raid by a lone aircraft — we sat tensed, waiting for our turn to come, until Tommy returned to put our minds at rest and rid us of the awful tension that was building up in the iron coffin.

Some were now saying they had smelt whiffs of petrol fumes coming from below our flooring, and the force of the explosion added to our suspicions that we carried fuel and bombs. That kind of unwanted knowledge did nothing to ease our worries or stiffen morale. It was some time before we heard that no prisoners had been on that particular ship; it had been one of our luckier days. The ship had been carrying fuel, bombs and the coolies whom the Japs had liberated then pressed into slavery. All were killed.

The *Amagi Maru* raised anchor at about 1750 hours on 20th April 1943, our sixth day in the hold. The atmosphere inside was foul with dirty bodies perspiring, the steel walls dripping in the heat and body lice indecently breeding. There was a fervent hope that we would benefit from a flow of fresher air once we got under way. Next day, a small number of men were allowed a half-hour period on deck; we knew that such a privilege could be taken from us by the nearest guard at the slightest provocation.

The guards placed themselves around the deck but on the whole we were not too closely policed and often a bored guard would attempt to start up a conversation, mostly in pidgin Malay with very imaginative gesticulations. Their motive was to lower our morale. It annoyed them that we managed to maintain morale despite everything.

We found that many Korean guards were apprehensive of their prisoners at first. That is not to suggest they were in any fear, rather that they could not understand our demeanour. Speaking their pidgin language with the help of waving arms and some 'special' gesticulations thrown in, they often resembled a short and very comical opera. We would be told:

'Ingris abis' (England finished), by their mighty German ally, and that Nippon was No 1, the English No 100, and the Americans were trailing very badly somewhere in the thousands. They also said that the Germans would take over England as a workshop, and the Japs would fight for a hundred years if need be and 'would never ever surrender'.

None of this was any good for morale as that nasty little doubt would always creep in, but it was never all one-sided. Our bright sparks would ask for progress of the war and the answers would always ensure a laugh under our breath.

When the guard was asked about Darwin, Australia, the conversation would go something like this. He would reply like a shot:

'Darwin bomb bomb. Nippon skoki bagus.' (Darwin bombed. Japanese air force very good.)

'Is London OK?' a prisoner would ask.

'Tida Lundun abis banya orang mati,' came back the reply. (No. London is finished. Many men dead.)

'What about New York?' hoping to catch him out.

'Damme damme America abis banya.' He was no lover of America! (Americans no good — all finished.)

The guard, with his sneering face and head held high, was most pleased with himself until a voice in exasperation called out:

'Bollocks!' in beautiful clear English.

The reply came back just as clearly:

'Ahso bolluks sama sama banya abis.' (Yes, bollocks the same, all finished.)

Backs quickly turned, hands to lips to avoid a burst of laughter. The guard could not understand why we smiled at such bad news — maybe he would ask Kasiyama, our interpreter, who would probably say the guard was correct anyway. This sort of conversational game was played many times, usually in working parties, to gain a longer *Yasumae* (rest), but always with care for you could soon end up in a one-sided punching match.

After one or two days at sea still heading eastwards, the first case of dysentery hit the hold, something we had been dreading in our packed situation. It was well known that the Japs were really frightened of disease — almost to the point of panic. We had little doubt that if an outbreak got out of control, the hatch would be battened down and stay that way. The sick were now shuffled into the centre of the floor, accompanied by the moans and groans of those who were walked upon or distressed, in a brave attempt at creating an isolation point. It was really only a gesture to those who were afraid of personal contact as no real benefit would be gained. With fuel and bombs below us, a possible dysentery epidemic inside and lurking submarines on the outside, what more could a man wish for?

The atmosphere in the hold became even more fetid, and those less able were clearly struggling as many expressed doubts about lasting the journey. We were hungry and suffering from malnutrition. Our first meal would appear at any time during the morning or the afternoon, and consist of a poor quality rice that only starving coolies would have eaten — so we did! The unpolished and dirty rice at least had a useful vitamin content. Containers were sent down, one of steamed rice, and the other of a watery soup made from pumpkins and seaweed. A bag of fish bones, head and tails included, often accompanied the soup for added flavouring. The bag would later be recovered and used again and again.

Our second meal would be of boiled rice which I can best describe as exactly like the flour paste my mum used to stick up wallpaper. No wonder it was called pap — it was nothing else but boiled rice with no salt or sugar to help it down. That menu remained unchanged each and every day, both on board ship and off it. Plenty of food had been available in Sourabaya, and for themselves the Japs had loaded live chickens and pigs, together with ample fresh fruit and dried fish. We always assumed that they gave their leavings to the pigs for they certainly wasted nothing on us except their dirty rice. The policy of just keeping us alive until the end of their work projects had well and truly started; once we had finished that work we became expendable.

It was our fourth day at sea, our tenth in the semi-darkness of the hold, and the smells became much worse as 250 men coughed, breathed and perspired together whilst the air seemed to stand still. Those well enough and nearest the Doc did what they could to help him administer the sick. Doc was most concerned that no one should die in the hold, so as not to alarm the guards. With nothing to do except try and pinch a few more inches of space from your chum, it was difficult not to become depressed. This was our first serious test on what would prove to be a long and difficult survival course. Our little combine would have a great need of each other, as life would have become unbearable without someone to share your troubles with.

It was about the twelfth night of our continuing misery and we were worrying more than ever about the length of the journey: if we continued travelling eastwards much longer we would run out of known Jap-held territory which would mean the unthinkable — we would sail right into Darwin. Was it possible the enemy could have landed in Australia? Was all our mickey-taking going to boomerang on us? Anything seemed possible in our mixed-up state of mind.

It was 30th April 1943 when we finally stopped and dropped anchor, causing another deafening crescendo of noise in the hold:

'Come on mate, pull yourself together.'

'Thank God, let's get out.'

'We've made it pal, we are there.'

'These ******** will be sorted out one day!'

We thought we had arrived at Haruku, our 'holiday' home. But life was never so easy. The stop was at Ambon Town on the island of Ambonia. There the Allied bombers were waiting to welcome us: the place was alive with the sounds of shore guns and dropping bombs. It was difficult to decide which was the worst — our own bombers or the enemy guards; most of us cared for neither. We were immediately instructed to get up on deck and leave our centre floor space clear for unloading, having first moved the sick onto the bamboo shelving around the hold.

We began unloading and as the first cargo came to light we were to see the first sling of citrus fruits, fresh vegetables and coconuts passing within inches of men dying from dysentery and malnutrition. In spite of a number of slappings and some swollen faces the Japs did not see the fruit that was thrown onto the shelving and they certainly would not enter the hold to check because of their fear of disease. We were now learning of another Japanese policy toward prisoners — to be 'worked' until they chose the time for us all to die.

The next stop was neither the last nor was it Haruku. In fact it was Amahai on the island of Ceram. The enemy had an outpost there and we were to unload yet more cargo. Not many of us felt fit enough to manhandle bombs and fuel, but we needed fresh air and had no other option.

Another ship I believed to be the *Kunitama Maru* had stopped alongside us with 1,000 Dutchmen on board. They appeared to be staying on Amahai.

Gunso Mori and his sidekick Kasiyama continued to make our lives unbearable.

'Offcer alle men worko, quicko', came the fiendish half-bawled, half-screamed call we would come to know so well — Blood had spoken. His leering face at the hatch opening repeated the cry every few seconds, promising that this was to be no Sunday school party. We hauled ourselves up and onto the deck wondering just what else life had in store. In spite of our short spells on deck during the arduous journey our legs were still reluctant to function, and the spirit was no more willing, but under the ever-watchful eyes of the guards, work commenced when the wooden flooring was lifted.

I could see the island a short way from the ship but there was no sign of a jetty or small boats to ferry ashore the cargo of fuel drums and bombs that now lay before our eyes. We wondered how we were expected to get this stuff ashore. During our earlier months of captivity we had learnt that the Japs did not understand the words 'cannot do' or 'impossible', and now we were to see a prime example of this. The petrol drums came first.

'Bloody hell, look at that lot! The bloody lot of us would have fried had a torpedo hit the ship,' came the exclamations as our cargo was revealed. Whilst still staring in disbelief the first drums were hauled out and pushed overboard, followed by a small party of guards. The swimmers headed for the drums, and taking one each, they swam them ashore, rolled them up onto the beach and stacked them. Our non-swimmers watched in fear and with nervous tension.

'Nippon soldier No 1 very good. Ingris, Hollander, sama sama speedo,' (English and Dutchmen do same quickly), came the cocky order with no regard for non-swimmers — it was go or be pushed!

Those who couldn't swim had already moved off towards the back of the crowd, but the sailors and swimmers didn't need telling twice. It was a heaven-sent opportunity to dip in cool water and wash some grime away — the chance did not come often. Some of the non-swimmers escaped to unload the drums and others went to stack them on shore. Borderline cases such as Ted and I had to take our chance with the rest and take a running jump.

The setting, a beautiful tropical island floating in a coral blue sea would have been the idyllic holiday home. But there was no time to dream, for moving amongst us the guards were voicing their battle crys,

'Banya speedo, orang lecas' (much speed, men hurry).

Orders would come in mixed languages, all with a clear meaning.

'Kono yaro, Ingris dame dame piggi.' (English stupid fools, no good, go.)

The water at this point was pleasantly calm, the drums were very supportive and, with many good swimmers around, the risk to non-swimmers was minimal. No problems arose for the four of us but another very good friend, Martin Oldfield was not so lucky.

This is how Martin remembered it forty years later:

'Like yourself Jim, I wasn't the best of swimmers and I well remember that, with the currents, the ship was turning slowly whilst at anchor. When I collected my first drum I found that I couldn't see very well over the top or ahead of me. Only after thinking it was a long time reaching the beach did I edge along the drum so as to see ahead. I also remember saying something rather blue — I was mortified and seemingly alone in the sea. I eased the drum around until it faced the island which was behind me — I had been paddling out to sea.'

At this point we agreed that he couldn't have drifted too far or he would have received a shot across his bows.

'I suppose I was only drifting out slowly but it was much too far for my liking,' replied Martin.

I don't mind admitting that I was also scared stiff, until I had that first trip behind me. I then made sure there would be no return trip, by malingering around the stacking point on the beach.

The whole of the exercise was pre-planned and it went without a hitch. Clearly it was not the first time the Japs had adopted this method. By the time the petrol was unloaded we looked for a well-earned rest. We knew it was not to be when we sighted a number of small boats arriving, whose cargoes of 500lb bombs also had to be unloaded and put ashore. They were packed in very rough boxes and all the prisoners who could still stand continued for more than thirty hours without food and with only brief breaks every four hours. It was incredibly hard work for us in our weakened condition to manhandle wet and slippery 500lb bombs from a ship onto a small boat.

Before we left Ceram were were transhipped onto a smaller craft and we knew then that we were not too far from our ultimate destination, Haruku. We were relived to see the back of the *Amagi Maru* — how were we to know that by our captor's standards we had completed a pleasure cruise?

6.   The Haruku Terror

The island of Haruku is in the Muluccas group, five degrees south of the equator and only five metres above sea level. It is sited south of Ceram between the islands of Ambon and Sapuru and its climate is very hot by day and cool to cold at night.

During our stop at Ceram or Ambon, there had been at least one ugly incident involving an airman in one of the other parties. A twenty-eight year old Geordie had been challenged by a trouble-making *gunso* for supposedly moving in the ranks. This infamous *gunso* was called 'Yellow Boots' in Jaarmarkt because of the yellow calf-length boots he wore. The boots were of the finest quality leather and he strutted around camp as though he were Hirohito; a real nasty piece of work. He had apparently pulled the Geordie out and given him a severe beating from which I know he did not recover. The same sadistic *gunso* perpetrated many more inhuman and criminal acts as we would later see.

After the short journey from Amahai we reached our destination. It was raining heavily — almost at monsoon levels — and getting dark at about 9-10pm. It looked as though we would have to stay on our floating hotel for the night. Of course, we should have known better than to apply logic to the situation; the Japs had no more respect for the weather than they had for us, and they immediately began to unload us like cattle. Maybe the guards were anxious to leave the ship for the comfort of their new barracks.

It was now 5th May 1943 and, like smugglers, we landed on that dark and stormy night by the light of a few hurricane lamps. Within minutes we were soaked to the skin and the clothes we stood up in were the only ones we possessed. The cold became intense as we shivered and shook — the irony was that we had prayed to leave the sea and now we wished to be back on board for the night.

Having landed, we found ourselves on sloping undrained swampland in secondary jungle undergrowth. The site was only a short distance from the sea and consisted of a number of half-built huts in a jungle clearing.

'Is this to be our promised land?' I asked Ted. 'Do you think this may only be a night stop?'

I really don't know how I expected him to know but I continued,

'Maybe they have to clear the ship quickly, so they dumped us here overnight.'

I wish I could recall the many things that were being said that night, though no doubt they were mostly unprintable! I thought it might be a partly-built *kampong* belonging to the island natives. How wrong could I be. Suddenly, from nearby could be heard the yapping voice of 'Tokyo Taff' (Kasiyama). No disrespect to our Welsh friends for that nickname but his accent was clearly Welsh not English — sorry fellows!

'All men yasumae, this is your new home,' said Kasiyama.

Home indeed! He had to be joking. If ever there was any danger of a mass suicidal uprising it must have been on that particular night. The anger and obscenities that pervaded the night air could not have been misunderstood by Kasiyama and still he remained totally unmoved, merely saying,

'The camp is not ready yet — tomorrow we can begin to complete the work.'

Kasiyama had read our message and he now quickly disappeared towards the ship. At that moment most of us had gone through enough and it was only common sense that kept many out of serious trouble.

First thoughts had to be for the sick people who were also unloaded into the cold and filthy weather. We were told to look after ourselves whilst others attended the sick. An inspection of the site by the CO and Senior Doctor Bruning, with the help of a couple of hurricane lamps, found a few places in half-finished huts where a little cover could be given to the worst cases. Our own little combine, not knowing what may creep or lurk in the nearby undergrowth, kept close to the waters' edge. No shelter was to be found so we huddled around the trunk of a coconut tree, doing our best to share the one waterproof we had. Instead of one person remaining reasonably dry, all four of us simply got a little less wet — but we had shared and that was all-important.

That night was amongst the worst I have ever suffered in all of my life, and many men were in a much worst state of health than myself. Meanwhile, the medical orderlies and others did their pitiful best for those dying or in desperate despair. Morale that night took another steep nose-dive — after spending fourteen ghastly days and nights at sea like rats in that iron trap, this night seemed to be the proverbial last straw.

Now saturated and freezing cold we did not fall in love with Haruku. From the extreme atmosphere of the hold to the wet freezing cold, many thought they had reached their limit of endurance. Some were wrong, for they would battle on each day and endure much more and still survive — if they were lucky. Somehow the night did pass; exhaustion allowed a few brief moments of sleep, only for us to waken feeling much worse.

It is almost impossible to describe the sight that greeted us at the break of dawn. In huddled clusters all around, sitting and laying in the middle of soaking wet and muddy undergrowth, we must have been a near perfect portrayal of man's inhumanity to man. It was at such times that the men were sorted from the boys, the good from the bad and the kind from the selfish. There were not too many boys; we were all growing up very quickly and from now on it would more than ever be a question of character and constitution. In the final analysis, the very will to live, for whatever reason, would decide our individual outcome. Now was the time when leaders were sought and judged, respected and obeyed or were found to be wanting and so disregarded. On Haruku we were fortunate to have a good leader, with at least two aides, who met every problem head on. Their task was a real and heavy burden, but only rarely do they receive suitable recognition.

The long bamboo huts had partly-built sides, and a gaping hole in the roof where the coconut trees still grew. The ground inside was unmade and undulating with nasty potholes and razor sharp coral rocks. Outside each hut a drain had been dug as a latrine trench; following the overnight rains they were full of water, and excrement left by the native labour force floated on the surface. 'The bastards will pay for this one day,' is a fair description of the most common threat being made.

That first night on land was, I believe the beginning of the downward journey into Boot Hill for many who would become its first occupants. Who was it that said:

> 'Things are only unbearable
> Until you are forced to bear them'?

About thirty men were now marked as being very ill, one of whom was our Geordie friend who had been beaten up by Yellow Boots earlier. The Japs brought along a few straw mats with which to cover the very ill — it was indeed one of their weaker moments. We welcomed the warm tropical sun to warm our bodies and dry out our soaked clothing; I suppose it was the one time we ever welcomed anything remotely connected with a 'rising sun.' At Haruku our combine of four pledged to be lifelong and firm friends, to lean on and help each other at all times. Many prisoners remember their own combines — our world was dominated by them and it was the nearest many would get to their own families.

> 'We could not tell the precise moment
> When our friendship was born.
> Like topping up your glass, drop by drop
> There is a moment when the last drop
> Runs over
> So it is after many kindnesses
> There is a time when your heart is full
> With love and respect for each other.'

Due to the continuing rains, it was twenty-four hours before the cookhouse staff of naval 'experts', using their own improvisations, produced our first food — boiled rice of course, what else? That first rice was soggy burnt pap — those lads had not used their cooking skills on the HMS *Electra* or HMS *Jupiter*, as they would have been keelhauled.

For the next few days we worked on the huts and still the rains came or were never far away. New drains were cut and formed around the huts so as to divert the water from the ground that we slept on. Owing to the reluctance of our captors to provide us with any suitable tools, our efforts were only partly successful and eventually local natives were brought in to advise and help.

The natives appeared to be of the same race as the Ambonese soldiers we had met in Sumatra — they were proud and loyal, quiet yet tough. Unlike most Asians their skin was an ebony black. They were well-proportioned and of a negroid appearance, suggesting African origins. Their life had been peaceful before being forced into an ugly and lasting change by 'outsiders'. We continued to make *bali-bali* bamboo shelving on which to rest. A better name would have been 'bug-bug' shelves — they were crawling!

The work progressed until the disastrous conditions on arrival improved a little. Then the Japs wasted no time and on 11th May 1943 our CO was ordered to provide two 600-man shifts to start building an airstrip — the reason for our being on Haruku.

The campsite was still very muddy and swamplike and we had not yet isolated the dysentery cases who badly needed more latrine trenches in close proximity, as each day the area became more fouled. A bamboo rail was placed along the length of these trenches for the sick to hold on to — but on more than one occasion a weakened man could not hang on, and would fall into those filthy trenches with their seething masses of large fat maggots. All this happened in full view of everyone else and we found it impossible to imagine anything more revolting and degrading, but it was all part of the exercise to humiliate us. In order to try and control the developing epidemic, we needed much more time and some help, yet the criminal lack of response from the Japs escaped all logic. A week or two longer working in the camp with suitable medicines and disinfectants would have paid real dividends for everyone in the long term. From this time forward the Japs were totally responsible for the deaths that followed so unnecessarily on Haruku.

Gunso Mori played God whilst his commandant, Lieutenant Kurishima, went into self-exile. Tokyo Taff (Kasiyama) crept around outside the huts during the dark hours, listening to our evil words then reporting them to his Big Brother. Major Anami (Goatee) may just as well have stayed in Tokyo with the *geisha* — he couldn't have cared less.

Mori set himself up as the soul and spirit of our camp and no other Jap or Korean ever dared challenge a single word. Slightly above average Japanese height, thick set and muscular, he was proud to think of himself as an extrovert. His voice had a peculiar chesty resonance to it, mostly very harsh, which used to its full was fear-inspiring. Yet on very rare occasions its owner was cordial and that same voice took on a coarse but purring sound. Being somewhat vain, he never missed an opportunity to show his brute physical strength. By no means stupid, he lived for and within a strict military code of very rigid disciplines which took no account of sadism — and even condoned it. It was said he was a veteran of Jap-China wars, where he supposedly won the equivalent of our Victoria Cross — The Order of the Chrysanthemum.

Mori had absolutely no time for thieves, liars, purveyors of deceit or malingerers, and woe betide anyone found guilty in 'his' court on any one account. The guilty could be Allied, native, or one of his own people; they were all the same to *Gunso* Mori. He would use the sick to the point of violating the humane code, and very often he would go far beyond that. Therefore, the only people he recognised as worthwhile were dedicated military morons. If you had any sense at all you simply tried your best to keep out of his way.

It is most important that this portrait of Mori, still indelibly imprinted on my mind, is understood because the man was destined to rule our lives in the foreseeable future — not the brightest of prospects.

Our CO had to make up the two working parties from those able to work, plus any volunteers. Our combine, having assessed the situation inside the camp, had agreed that we should get outside at every opportunity while we were able. The second working party had to reach the work site before the first was released, so for long periods there were no really fit men in the camp to help with the sick. Progress to improve the camp conditions came almost to a halt.

On my first walk to the drome I remember being very tired on arrival — it had seemed about three or four miles. We soon found we were scheduled for hard labour and that the only beautiful Japanese word was 'Yasumae' (rest). We all agreed that doing that every day was going to be tough, but we would sooner crawl there than stay in camp.

My first two days were spent helping survey the site and marking out. Those early days could have been much worse but the Japs had not got themselves organised and their soldiers were doing some preparatory work. Our CO at once requested that both parties be allowed to go out together as one shift of 1,200 men — it was refused as usual without consideration: no one should dare question a Jap order, least of all an officer who had allowed himself to be taken a prisoner. It was going to be tough on some of our officers, though not all extended themselves.

On about 12th May, the first man died on Haruku. Each day that followed brought more deaths — victims of malnutrition or dysentery. The sickness rate galloped along until by the end of May 1943, the death toll had reached eighty. The Geordie lad, Bob Green, had died from the effects of his beating by Yellow Boots; had treatment been made available he would not have died.

It was now becoming more difficult to find enough so-called fit men to meet the demands of the drome. Our captors remained immovable and totally unreasonable, indicating a culture I should hate to confuse with civilisation as we know it. The more we learnt of their ways the less we were surprised by their ignorance of simple humane rights and needs. Sadism would prove to be their first commandment and their most evil characteristic.

On the first *Tenko* after Mori was told the full quota could not be met, the officers were lined up alongside us and slapped about the head. Being 'slapped' by the Japs should not be confused with the playful slaps that may be exchanged by Westerners. It consisted of a clenched fist thrown from the thigh with maximum force ending up on the face or skull with rapid repetitive movements. Beatings came along regularly and cost very little, as cheap as a bat of an eyelid sometimes. If you were unable to take the beating, or went down purposely thinking your attacker would desist, then you had made your first mistake, for then the boot would go in with obvious joy. If you could avoid flinching or showing any sign of distress you may 'save face', which, however you understand it, was their second commandment.

On occasions a 'toughie' stood his ground and would glare directly into the attacker's eyes, who then sniggered and walked away, realising he wasn't going to get any satisfaction, but those men were few and far between, and anyway, you could never be sure of their next reaction — at all times they were imponderable and deceitful.

May 24th and my 21st birthday brought me no presents and very little consolation, for on that day I lost another 242 Squadron friend, Ted Belsham from Surrey. Another friend tried to commit suicide.

By 12th June 1943, there were over 300 dysentery cases tightly packed on uncovered bug-ridden bamboo slats. During the week of the 1st to the 7th, 42 men died (31 British and 11 Dutch). The grand total now stood at 132 in only five weeks. Most died at night like candles being snuffed out, quietly and without too much resistance. The situation was not pleasing the enemy and on 14th June all 'walking' sick were specially paraded on a *Tenko*.

Our two nasty jailers, Blood and Slime, were instigating their new-style *Tenko*. All the sick who could stand, including those with leg ulcers, chest problems, severe neuritis, beriberi and the many symptoms of malnutrition, were on parade. It was no use leaving anyone behind in a hut hoping to cover for them as the guards would be flying around, joyfully looking for victims as they brandished their personal length of bamboo. Mori and Kasiyama, in their usual bawdy fashion, went viciously along the *Tenko* lines hitting over the head anyone they considered fit enough to reach the drome. Only when their quota was finally reached would they dismiss the *Tenko*. This action was to demonstrate the way the game would be played by them and that we should take notice. One might well ask, 'Where was their commandant?'

The simple answer is he didn't show up very often — Mori alone ran the show and his maxim was really quite simple:

'If you bleed and die then you are with honour. If you are only sick and die then you are dishonoured and useless.'

We decided our original choice was correct — to keep going to the drome for as long as we could stand, seeking extra scraps of food from whichever source we might find. Mori meant every word he said and, according to his beliefs and code of practice, I suppose he was generally honest. Some thought him typical of the Samurai warrior as he would follow their code whenever possible. Maybe this code of the Bushido was not intended for his class but he would show it all the respect he could muster.

> 'We are the Knights of the Bushido
> Of the order of the rising sun.
> We do not execute at sunset
> But at sunrise.'

Our combine managed to get on a working party in the jungle — we were to be eight or nine stone lumberjacks! If I remember correctly the party was in the charge of the 'Mad Monk'. He was a guard who expressed everything by gesticulation in the fervent hope he would be misunderstood, in which case he would feel justified in punishing his prisoners. It was like the panel game *What's my line*? Upon our arrival at the work site he would hold his arms open wide to indicate a diameter, then he would point to the ground if he wanted a hole to be dug or point to a tree that he wanted felled — in each case the job had to be done to the diameter he had first indicated. Guessing was straightforward in the jungle as there were not too many options. Anywhere else, however, where there were many possible meanings to many different signs, half the party would fall prey to his slappings for not understanding.

Felling a tree wasn't always too difficult if the party was made up of crafty and cunning lads who quickly learnt the dodges. First we would cut a trench around the tree, maybe six feet away, until we exposed its roots, working as slowly as we dared. The work area around the tree had to be kept as small as possible so as not to accommodate all the party; that way, some worked whilst others enjoyed a little rest between stints. When we were forced to finally expose the roots, whenever the Mad Monk turned away, we would 'accidentally' push loose earth back into the trench so that when compelled to dig, it was nice easy going — it all became a work of art.

Some guards were rather thick, and the odd one was lazy, so it would take them ages to cotton on to our low production rate. Sometimes, though, a guard would become so angry at our poor work rate that he would scream,

'Ingris tida bagus! Mari sini siya keraja.' (English no good, come out, I work.)

He would then jump into the hole and he would dig like hell! As long as we showed our appreciation he would dig out half the hole for us and, believe me, every little rest was invaluable.

Occasionally a little extra rice would be granted for the drome workers — this rice was not additional, but was taken from the sick and the camp workers. Whenever possible it was returned to its rightful place and no one complained.

Punishment within the camp became much more frequent as the guards on their random walks through the camp would assault anyone within striking distance. The 'reasons' were pitiful: for not bowing at the right time, whether or not you had seen the guard; or if you had saluted (bowed), for not doing so at the correct angle. If all this was faultless then we were accused of not holding the bow long enough.

It was a deliberate plan of harassment in an attempt to make the camp a most inhospitable place to be.

Each week that passed became more miserable and difficult to cope with; hunger, sickness and pain, filth and despondency were the order of each day. Though some inner voice would still say, 'Don't let these bastards get you down', another would argue, 'Why bother? You'll never return home. Take the easy way out and just give up trying.'

When arriving back from the drome at night we were just as likely to walk into a slapping at the camp guardroom, usually on some set pretext. I know that I seemed to walk into more than my rightful share because the guards would insist I was abusing them, simply because, as I talked, I often looked in their direction.

The harassment inside camp continued until the only safe place to be was in Hut No 1, by now known as the 'death hut'. It was the one place those brave Japs didn't dare go near, let alone walk inside — they were really frightened of disease. Often, in the ordinary sick huts, men had to make a superhuman effort to lift themselves into a sitting position simply to salute the lowest ignoramous wearing a Jap uniform. Some guards would even climb onto the bamboo shelf and clip a sick and helpless man for being slow to respond. At such times it was extremely difficult to discipline oneself to not react physically or even to adopt an aggressive attitude, which was exactly what they wanted of course.

Our CO asked Lieutenant Kurishima, whenever he could reach him, to allow us to erect a sea latrine on a wooden jetty. The request was always denied. We were not even allowed to wash ourselves or our eating utensils in the sea. We would be told very often,

'Damme damme banya Nippon sakit' (No good it make all Nippon sick) — come to think about it, not a bad idea!

At this time there were one or two men wandering around camp, living in some fantasy world and asking

'Where am I, where are we going?'

We always found time to understand these few lads who would very soon opt out.

The starvation diet of the same small tin (cup size) of boiled rice and the same small measure of steamed rice with a watery soup made from pumpkins and cucumber, made up our everyday intake of food. Everyone was quickly weakening — every day the fit became weak, the weak grew weaker and others would die. The water being brought in from the nearby stream now showed unhealthy signs of pollution from our camp drains. The situation was crazy and so illogical, for if the workforce continued to die at an ever-increasing rate, the Jap work project would remain incomplete. They may just as well have sunk us in Sourabaya harbour, as someone had earlier suggested, but still they would not listen. We were now feeling the need to remind ourselves that

'To remain strong at heart
Do not notice how weak
Your best friend is'

A visiting Jap doctor was challenged by Doctor Bruning over serious matters and the Jap answered:

'I am a soldier first; I can do nothing. As a doctor I can understand.'

I believe we would call that two-faced, and ample proof that the Military ruled their roost. Toward the end of 1943 there were 400 sick men with 150 near to death. Even so, 30 or 40 walking sick were taken from the 400 and slapped before being made to work on their knees within the camp.

My good friend Dick Keefe of 242 Squadron had some responsibility, along with an RAF officer, for the burial parties. The officer would say a short prayer as we had no padre. They were being kept busy at Boot Hill and much of the work was unpleasant, but they did what they could for our dead friends and comrades. Ted, Joe, Bill and I had managed to avoid the worst of things, or so we thought. I didn't know any loners, though there were one or two: they would not last long without the help of a friend at some stage. We four were becoming unhappy with our lot and it was all too easy to give in to depression.

The island was made up of secondary jungle growing from a volcanic subsoil, sandy terrain and coral rock. At the island's centre were two hills and we were to build the airstrip at the highest point. Our first task was to remove the two peaks, putting the material into the existing hollow between the two hills, thus providing a level strip. The bulk of the work was apparently to be carried out by that well-known worker 'Manuel Labour', for there were no mechanical aids. On our second day at the drome, we were issued with tools, if 'tools' be the correct description for such an absolute load of rubbish. Obviously the Japs intended to ignore the words of Churchill:

'Give us the tools and we will finish the job.'

The selection was unbelievable: small twelve-inch cold chisels, hammers possibly 2lb in weight and spades which I assume were cut from fifty-gallon drums. There were also other forms of native tools such as the chunkel and more popular sack with its bamboo pole, but all the tools were more suited to digging a garden rather than hacking through the island's dense and rocky terrain. The bamboo pole and sack was called a *tanga* or *moko-moko* — both names have been used — and we would all become well-acquainted with it. We were not impressed with our task, but were still pleased, for it meant that the war would probably be over before we finished their airstrip and became fodder for the jungle roots and creatures. It would surely be likened to building the pyramids; our enemy had the labour of both 'white slave' and 'coolie' — if they kept them alive long enough! A low-cost diet and free labour and housing ensured a cheap, if not quality, airstrip — or one very large cemetery.

Pleased to be out of camp, we all dived in for the best of the tools — judged only by how little work the tool would demand. The speed at which the sacks and the bamboo poles disappeared had the four of us non-plussed, but most lads had worked out the purpose of them — we were certainly slow off the mark in those earlier days. It was only possible to carry a limited amount of soil in a sack which would be carried on the shoulders with the bamboo passed through two rope handles, rather like a carrier bag. So two men would, at worst, be compelled to carry a fully-loaded sack all day. How heavy the load would feel depended on a man's fitness.

We all wondered how the Japs expected us to build an airstrip with that load of useless tools. I didn't think that *we* would be the ones to finish it — to last the distance we would need meat and vegetables, let alone steam rollers and bulldozers. Men could be heard saying, 'They must be bloody nutcases.' Then we would remember how far those 'nutcases' had come, more or less living off conquered lands. We should have recognised the lengths to which they would go to achieve their objectives: Kasiyama once said:

'America forced us into war by refusing us access to vital raw materials in the East.' He was not far from the truth.

Each day at *Tenko* the smaller working parties would be selected, leaving the rest of our workforce to be worker ants on the drome. Before leaving camp in a party someone would invariably fall for a slapping as we scrambled for what we believed to be the best jobs. For the first few weeks the four of us went to the drome without finding a decent job but we did find that it was more pleasant working together in a foursome on the *tanga*'s — two breaking rock and shovelling, the other two on the pole and sack. We soon learnt the tricks of this job. When the guard wasn't looking we would stop long before the sack was full. All we had to do was pray that a guard at the other end did not watch the emptying. On a few occasions, we would load so much that the bamboo would bend almost to a 'U' shape in great danger of snapping. The guard would invariably say, 'Ahso banya bagus.' (Ah very good.) Then, with luck, he would disappear for a while, leaving us in peace.

We became real experts of the slow, slow march — our style was one step forward and the occasional two back, with eyes and ears primed for any red alert. The longer we took to reach the other end and unload, the longer the rest we were able to gain for our friends. After a time we would change places, providing the guard didn't stick his oar in. I imagine a loaded sack would weigh around half to three-quarters of a hundredweight; later it felt like a ton, as each day became more difficult. The full heat of the tropical sun was no help as it seemed to squeeze the last drop of fluid from our already weakened bodies. Like others before us we decided to look for the easier jobs which were now becoming far fewer in number.

At the break of dawn we would be called to *Tenko*, often having just won the nightly battle of the bamboo bugs and settled in an uneasy sleep. I suppose the hollow tube-like bamboo made a natural warm home and breeding ground for those awful bugs, which were as large as ladybirds and with a hell of a bite. It was remarkable the things you would suffer to stay alive. Eighteen months ago the very thought of sharing with so much vermin would have turned my stomach, but we were now reaching the depths of degradation — the limit to which man could adjust in his fight for survival.

So *Tenko* was called, and we rushed to complete early chores trying not to be late. Those who had water stored in an old tin from the previous rains were the minority who could wash the sleep from their eyes. There was no water in camp except for that carried in for the sick, by the semi-sick camp workers, from the nearby stream, therefore we stayed dirty unless a way was found to wash whilst on an outside working party. Most men had only a shirt and shorts — or even only shorts — in which they worked and slept, so it was little wonder that body lice chose to live and breed in waistbands. No dressing time was needed in our social structure so men just dragged themselves off the bamboo to start another day, just like yesterday and with no more hope. We would barely have time to push down our measure of rice pap before the howling *banzai* calls would round us up to take another walk to the drome — just another day feeling that all the world was against us.

The walk through that secondary jungle was a burden in itself and we often wondered how many more trips we could make. There was never a more ragged bunch than ourselves as, with only two guards, one in front and the other at the rear, we would shuffle our way to the drome. The column of men, two or three abreast and in some cases totalling hundreds of men, would wind its way like a huge snake, twisting and turning around the many bends. For long periods neither guard was visible and anyone could have slipped away into the undergrowth, but it was meaningless as there was nowhere to go. I suppose it could have been likened to Alcatraz or, with our unwanted company, maybe Devil's Island.

Many things would happen along the way, such as slappings for stopping to help a friend in trouble as men collapsed. Some brave and crafty lads would break ranks when the guards were out of sight, in order to reach a nearby plantation, a single tree carrying something hopefully edible or simply some jungle roots — anything that resembled food was treasured and sought after. A man could not afford to be of a nervous disposition or in poor health when attempting such excursions, so numbers were limited. If sighted away from the main column, no one doubted that any guard would shoot to kill without any compunction whatsoever. If anyone met their death this way, the Japs would simply alter the total column of their figures. It was my desire, most of the time, to ensure that No 624 stayed on their list to tell the tale. Men who could not manage to reach the drome under their own steam were always helped by a pal — there was never any need to ask as the nearest able man would hold out his helping hand. So on and on it continued; if you kept going then you were indeed fortunate, but no more tough or brave than the fallen, simply a little more determined, pig-headed or downright naive, as I was.

As time passed, the situation in camp began to get out of control, and still the Japs had no idea of its magnitude, or else they chose to remain totally indifferent. They were still prepared to hand out regular beatings at the slightest provocation, the sick being no exception, and they continued to turn out the walking sick. If anyone's health improved as a result of turning out on parade, then a doctor would be punished. The odd scrounger and a few others would benefit from the psychological uplift of being with men more fit than themselves, who showed them it was better to work as long as possible.

The deaths continued into early June 1943 which made us even more determined to drag ourselves to the drome in an effort to survive. At night we would throw ourselves down, dead beat and no doubt squashing our many unwelcome bed-mates at the same time, give a relaxing sigh, then curse the guards, especially if some booty had been taken from us at the guardroom. Then we would find out what had happened in other working parties:

'Did you get anything in?'

'Not much, a couple of ketela roots and some leaves.'

'Did you see the tree near your job that has either nuts on or small fruit?'

'I think so, anyway its worth checking tomorrow.'

We had to be careful as an earlier party finding such a tree ate the nuts from it and then became very ill — the nuts were castor oil! In their condition it was far from being funny, but I think most of us still had a little smile at the episode.

Earlier in the evening we would have stood in a queue with hundreds of others to collect our meal of steamed rice (complete with weevils) and water pumpkin soup. A fifty-gallon drum holding the rice was closely guarded by the 'cook' and his 'minder', who were often somewhat fatter than ourselves. A carefully-measured issue was made to each man, closely watched by all within sighting distance to ensure there were no obvious favourites. Another lad would be posted at the back of the queue to prevent anyone from queueing twice, except of course his friends if and when they could manage it. The second queue, now almost legendary, is known to ex-Fepow's as the 'lagi queue'. Usually, though, the double-queuers would wait in vain as only slight mistakes in issue left anything over. Anyway, most of us thought it better to live with the hunger and retain some dignity, rather than push and shove for a few more almost useless grains of rice.

The effects of malnutrition lead to a low resistance to disease, and together with the filthy conditions it meant that many took the easier way out by giving up their unequal fight. We had received only half a cake of soap each on our arrival in May, and we had been promised the other half in November, six months later.

We would arrive back at night after a strength-sapping day, suffering from the run's enough to frighten us. Often after a night-long fight with mosquito's and bugs we would just drop off to sleep only to be awakened again with the runs. We would have to go out into the cold night air in bare feet and across the now muddy and polluted terrain. We had to pick a way carefully to the latrine trench in semi-darkness making sure we found the handrail of bamboo, to prevent us falling in! There was never any paper, only a bucket of unclean water from which you had to attempt to cleanse yourself. Imagine a really sick man, only strong enough to stand, who had to make that run fifty or more times during one unhappy day and night.

Many would spend a night in this way and then be forced to go to the drome as soon as daylight came and until they dropped. By the next morning some would be unable to continue without help and would be compelled to report as overnight sick. The sick parade was taken at the same time as the morrning *Tenko*. Most of us fought extremely hard to avoid having to make this choice of work or sick, for it could well be the beginning of the end.

Our combine now decided it was time to reassess our responsibilities to each other. It was agreed that Ted and I would scrounge, or take, what we could from anywhere, except from other prisoners. This meant that Ted and I had to always keep our eyes open for the infrequent but valuable opportunity of gain. Bill and Joe would do any bartering inside and outside of camp, whenever we had the means. Dealings would mainly be with natives, putting both parties at some risk for it was strictly forbidden, and there was also the risk that not all natives would hold their tongue if questioned. Our trading would generally take place around the drome site where the native could melt away into the jungle leaving us to carry the booty. The four of us had a few valuables with which to barter, which we had held on to as long as possible — now they would have to go in exchange for the fruit and coconuts we badly needed. By comparison with others, our combine was still solvent, and even wealthy. It may not sound very much but when those around you have nothing, then even a little wealth brings power, and that will never change.

One morning at *Tenko* Joe and I struck it lucky; without any effort we had landed a good job in a decent party — we were put in charge of the tool shed on the drome. It was a small hut just off the strip in a shady spot and handy for the trading *benjo* in the undergrowth. Our job was to issue and repair tools, then collect and check them in each night — we had suddenly become *Tuan besar's* (big shots).

The guard in charge was 'Little Henry' who was just about my match at 5'2". He looked so young and innocent, that we gave him the nickname of *Ju-Hatchi* (eighteen). As guards go we found him reasonable, although it was most foolish to trust any one of them as they all could, and did, fly off the handle in a flash. It seemed to suit his ego to be in charge of a couple of short prisoners who did not tower over him and I should have appreciated my luck. He liked to chat a little from time to time using our mixed bag of languages and gesticulations which suited me fine. Joe and I were with him for some days until my tongue got me into trouble.

None of our combine had found a soft number before and Henry, when it suited him to do so, would give us his unwanted food or the occasional cigarette. When fighting a battle against starvation, the first lesson to learn is how to swallow your pride and accept what is offered. Only when the stomach shrinks and ceases to want, or maybe cannot take, food are you near the starvation level. So we would always carry our booty bag or tin in which to store whatever we were given or managed to pick up — anything thought to have a vitamin content would do. Our greatest successes would be the roots of ketela or tapioca, certain green leaves and the occasional cucumber or chilli. Now and again an apparent good find would turn sour on us such as when the old outer skin of certain roots contained enough arsenic to almost kill!

From our tool shed job it was easy to trot off to the *benjo* (with permission) and do a crafty deal without too much risk. Most of the natives were sympathetic for they, too, were being subjected to most unpleasant changes under their new masters. When Little Henry was away for a while we would slip into the undergrowth one at a time searching for roots and nuts, and always hoping for fruit. It really was our best job so far and often we could collect enough green leaves for the four of us, a worthwhile risk, but like all good things it came to its end. Usually, though, it was the guard that terminated our contracts, not a stupid prisoner like myself.

When my friend on the *tanga*'s had said: 'Jim, you never stop talking for long,' I had no reason to expect Little Henry would have the same reason for 'sacking' me.

The war seemed a million miles away but we always kept an ear open to catch any news or rumour. In one of my duller and talkative moments, I decided to go to work on Little Henry and find out if he knew anything worthwhile. We were sitting on the ground enjoying a short rest and I was doodling away, scratching in the dry sandy earth with a stick, when I got carried away. To the best of my ability I started to scratch out the shape of Australia and mark on it the position of Darwin. Little Henry, in a fairly placid mood, sat quietly watching me. In the usual mixture of Japanese and Malay, by this time a practised art, I made my start. I indicated a 'Betsy' (Jap bomber) flying over Darwin and then said to him:

'Nippon skoki banya bagus, bomb bomb Darwin.' (Japanese airforce very good, bomb Darwin.)

Warming to me at once, Henry came straight back with:

'Ahso wakara.' (Yes understood.) A grunt and a big smile followed then he continued, 'Banya orang Australie mati.' (Many Australians dead.)

Henry was going to be OK, so I would continue our chat over a number of rest breaks — that was all I intended to do. I played it crafty, making out I was sad and upset by his news, and then I thought enough for today, as I knew he would talk. Tomorrow I would tackle him again at our break time, asking questions on the same topic to see if he told the same tale.

That evening, the lads brought in their tools then we grouped for the *Tenko* before leaving for camp. Some days we would be searched, so those with something to hide would stand at the back hoping that only the front rank would be searched, if any. The guard would already have been sussed as a known 'badee' or a 'relative goodee'. If the former, we would either dump the booty to collect later, or else take a chance. Either way, we were still likely to be searched at the camp guardroom and there was nowhere really safe to hide anything when only wearing shorts and some peculiar headgear — it was just a game. Any guard could have found something if he tried so in order to 'save face' for not being bothered about it, all looted food items had to be out of his obvious sight.

In earlier days Ted had tried putting some native tobacco in the hollow of a bamboo he was supposedly using as a crutch. It was found when the guard decided Ted could walk unaided. Having no reason to suspect anything, he playfully tapped Ted a couple of times on the head with it — imagine the nervous tension! Then he bashed it on the nearest rock before throwing it away and, in mid-flight, the tobacco decided to fall out, and the playing stopped.

The next morning, back on the drome with Little Henry and his tool shed, we issued tools and made a few repairs until our *yasumae* time came around: time for the second round of the battle. I re-drew my map and asked:

'Nippon go doko guntai?' (Jap army, where are they now?)

I thought he would never understand that gibberish, and that he may well object to the question, but Little Henry wasn't daft, and he came straight back at me with:

'Nippon guntai Australie Darwin sino.' (Japanese army in Australia, Darwin is dead.)

I then made my classic *faux pas*. What Little Henry had said contradicted yesterday's story — the Japs could not have bombed Darwin one day and be already entrenched there the next. Instead of biting my tongue at this inconsistency, I decided to be clever and score a few points over Little Henry:

'Wakari-nai,' (I don't understand.) I replied, then continued, 'Kino skoki bomb bomb Darwin. Nina Nippon guntai Darwin?' (Yesterday you say Japs bomb Darwin, so now all Japs dead?)

I had committed an unforgivable crime against his person by causing him to badly lose face. Surprisingly, he didn't properly assault me there and then. Joe, who had been watching us without realising what I had done, figured Little Henry had blown his top with me for dragging out the rest time. Henry walked over in a supercilious manner and trod all over the map, kicking the earth in all directions, shouting,

'Keraja lecas speedo!' (Work and fast.)

When I told Joe he said:

'You stupid bugger, Jim, you've done it now. You take the mickey and lose us the best job we've ever had, and you are lucky to settle for that.'

I didn't need to be told that another 5'5" chap would be replacing me in the morning. I knew I had let the whole combine down badly and I racked my brains wondering how I could put things right and make good my blunder.

'Sorry Joe, it was a fool thing to do and I should have known better.'

As an afterthought I continued:

'Maybe we can get Ted in my place in the morning.'

As long as Henry didn't see me around and his numbers were OK, I was sure he wouldn't worry, so Ted and I changed places on *Tenko* next morning whilst I kept out of Henry's sight. It worked and they went off, no problem. I was back on the *tanga*'s with Bill Pollock, having tried to make amends.

Already six months had passed on Haruku and we had lived daily on the two cupfuls of rice and the watery soup; at this rate another six months would probably be our limit of endurance. In the evenings we talked and moaned about our lot, often in a loud aggressive tone, when really we should have remembered that Tokyo Taff could be skulking around outside listening to our every word; that disgusting and treacherous piece of scum told Mori so many lies it was unbelievable. He caused so many men to be punished unjustly. On the other hand, there was a seldom-seen *gunso* in their medical branch called Fujioka who would never use Kasiyama as his interpreter as he didn't trust him.

Apart from a brief rest our evenings were spent visiting sick friends or simply chatting together. One evening whilst on a visit to a friend I was beckoned over by a medical orderly who told me:

'Jim, there is a chap in Hut No 1 asking for you,'

I couldn't think who that could be so I asked if I could go in and see him. The orderly said he would arrange it for me one evening.

I had visited Hut No 1 only once before, and promised myself I would not repeat the visit except for very close friends. How on earth any man could volunteer to help out in places like that is way beyond my comprehension; those doctors and their orderlies were the very salt of the earth. It was often said that no one ever came out of Hut No 1 alive — but that was not quite true. Usually, though, the next resting place on from Hut No 1 was Boot Hill.

I remember that the 'death hut' (No 1) stank to high heavens as all the patients were at the dying stage or no-hopers. The orderlies continued to lift 'skeletons with skin' over wooden buckets or else they slipped a tin plate under a body that could not be moved. Having washed a body and its sleeping space the emaciated man was rested for only a very short period of time before the same operation began all over again throughout the length of the hut. There was little wonder no Jap ever stepped foot inside. Their crass brutality did not provide them with that sort of courage, and they found it easier to kill than to save life.

At night that hut was allowed one hurricane-type lantern but oil for it was severely rationed, so that when the moon was bright the oil had to be saved. At night it was difficult to judge whether a man had died without clambering up onto the bamboo shelf and looking directly into his face.

The man I had been called in to see was Pat McGrogan a 'local' for me and one of the few lucky survivors of Hut No 1. He was to join the first sick draft back to Java — only to find himself having another similar battle to survive in Sumatra. He would tell you that Sumatra was no better than Haruku, and was possibly even worse due to the dense jungle terrain. If that was so then he and others of his ilk certainly deserved to survive both places. Today we remain good friends and the only two survivors of our ten 'locals' who were on Haruku island.

Pat McGrogan had an orderly friend named Paddy McQuade in Hut No 1. Let him tell you about Paddy in his own words, after having kept it to himself for forty years.

In those early days at Jaarmarkt camp, the chaps of 84 Squadron stuck together, sleeping in the same hut, going in the same working parties and generally sharing what little they had. As time went on we noticed that a slightly-built, bearded and somewhat unkempt individual, always attached himself to us. I suppose in some measure we resented it; not yet knowing any better, we were inclined to make superficial judgements. We were prepared to accept that, because the man looked scruffy, or scruffier than us, he was not as good as ourselves. Anyway, he continued to stay with us and eventually was accepted as being one of us.

He was, of course, an Irishman, who had come over to England in the thirties hoping to find work. Unable to do so he joined the RAF in 1936 — I suppose it was his last desperate attempt to find himself a meal ticket. When we later became firm friends he told me his name was William McQuade, known as 'Paddy'. He was born in Derry, Northern Ireland, and his sole surviving relative was his married sister.

When we went to Haruku Paddy was one of the party. Shortly after arriving there, what can only be described as a tidal wave of dysentery hit us. Paddy could not be found anywhere around, either in camp or up on the drome. Eventually he was discovered working as a volunteer medical orderly in the middle of the very worst cases. The Japs, as we know, were always in mortal fear of disease so they fenced off Hut No 1 from the remainder of the camp. Men who were most desperately ill were placed in that hut; that is where Paddy had selected to work. He remained there until we returned to Java from Haruku. I learnt at first hand how Paddy gave all his time, energy and his inspiration to those in that dreadful hut, irrespective of colour or creed.

My turn came to be struck down, to be amongst the unfortunates whose only possible chance of prolonging their lives for a day or a week lay in people like Paddy McQuade. The ugliness and hopelessness of that situation had to be seen to be believed and appreciated. The realisation that men were prepared to administer others in such conditions, with little or no regard for themselves, filled me with admiration. Since I recovered I have realised just how much they had to do; it's almost unbelievable that such men exist.

There is little wonder they called it the 'death hut' — bodies were laid on the bamboo shelves covered in their own excreta. They had ulcerated legs and many other sores, mouths wide open with dozens of horse flies and bluebottles in attendance. Maggots would often emerge from each and every orifice, crawling over their bodies, and all the men could do was lay there in filth and cry out for help. These were men who not many months before were perfectly healthy and happy 'middle or working class' people and they were now being needlessly murdered by the Japs who never came forward with constructive help of any sort. Words were not enough to describe the men who undertook this caring work on Haruku; most were dedicated yet amongst them Paddy stood out. He worked hard through his shift never taking time off for himself and the only rest he did take was when he slept.

After his shift was finished he would return after the briefest rest and would then administer his own brand of nursing therapy — persuading, bullying, cajoling and pleading; whatever it took to ensure the patient would respond to him in some way to signify he had not yet given up all hope. That seemed to be Paddy's main aim 'to keep alive the spirit that may keep him alive' without which he would certainly die. What price then was our earlier judgement of Paddy, that in our eyes he did not quite match up to ourselves? It was us who were wrong. I recall that when I first went into the 'death hut' his reaction was so typical of him:

'Jaasus Pat, what are you doing in here? I'll see to you when I've finished with this other fellow.'

After he had cleaned the other fellow and made him comfortable he came back to me.

'Now let me give you some good advice Patrick — keep on your feet if it kills you because it is the only way you can leave here alive.'

Real Irishman's advice, but good, and I tried to follow it to the letter. I am convinced that he is the sole reason I am here today.

Fortunately I was able to leave Haruku with Paddy still looking after me. We stayed in Cycle camp, Batavia, from where we were sent to Sumatra to work on a railway at Pakenbaru, the horrors of which were at least equal to those publicised about the Kwai. In due course Paddy and I were separated.

A few weeks from the end of the war I was returned to a base camp in Sumatra suffering from cerebal malaria. When I had sufficiently recovered to walk about I went to work as an orderly with another friend, Taff Tucker. Imagine my surprise and feelings when Paddy arrived with a party of 'incurables' — this time he was a patient. Paddy was aware that he was going to die and he had already accepted the fact quietly and calmly. Taff and myself, together with a Catholic Padre, did everything we could for Paddy. At that time we could obtain eggs and chicken plus other nourishing foods which we tried to feed him. Two weeks *after* the war ended Paddy finally passed away, and I have never known to this day the cause of his death, nor have I forgotten him.

Paddy McQuade left this world with even less than he had when he arrived in England to seek his fortune; he had given more to his comrades than can be measured in wealth.

If ever a man was a Saint then may Paddy rest in peace for he was that man . . .

7.   Must We All Die?

By the end of July 1943 the death toll was 250; a totally useless and unnecessary waste of life brought about by a race still operating a feudal culture of the sixteenth century. In little more than two months and from the original total of 2,060, we had 250 dead and approaching 1,000 ill, and there was still no sign of any constructive help from our captors. Not surprisingly, we wondered and believed that we were all ultimately intended as victims; it was a thought that lived with us day in and day out.

Then, like the proverbial light at the end of the tunnel, a welcome sign appeared. As if by magic, all work at the drome stopped which gave life to many rumours. The continuing battle by our CO and Dr Bruning to enlighten Mori and his sidekick had at long last paid some dividend, albeit temporarily. It was already too late to expect a camp clean-up to save very many without the appropriate medicines, but it was a step in the right direction.

The day before work stopped at the drome was not without its trauma, as our officer in charge that day would vouch. In our drome party, a guard was spitefully filling sacks for the *tanga* to the maximum instead of leaving the prisoners to it. The strong bamboo bent almost double into a 'U' shape as we trundled along under the heavy burden. It was bad enough having to carry it in the state we were in, and even worse knowing that if the bamboo snapped before you reached the other end there would be trouble, as the two carriers would be held responsible for the careless handling of the Emperor's possessions.

The whole charade had, of course, been set up for the ultimate slappings: at one end a guard creates the weight problem whilst at the other his mate takes unfair retribution. Our officer for the day also fell foul of them on this occasion, as he was responsible for our gross incompetence in breaking one or two bamboos. This was about the only entertainment the Koreans ever got. They were interesting, enigmatic and comical, yet very brutal and always as imponderable as their masters, and therefore dangerous. They were most certainly non-hedonistic, unless they considered this to be a pleasure.

Each day passed with regular and boring monotony accompanied by a fierce sun which reflected and glared unbearably from the coral rock directly into unprotected eyes; I sensed this was going to be my major problem. Each day passed unbelievably slowly before it was time for the going home *Tenko*, when the guard on our trail back to camp was often 'Gentleman Jim', yet another mixed up Jap. He was forever making noises that sounded like 'Ahso ha ha, ahso ha ha, OK ga, ahso ha ha', ad infinitum. We never knew if he was laughing, agreeing or rollicking us, and it was all too easy to fall foul of him.

On this particular day after the *Tenko* had been completed we headed back for camp. When we reached somewhere outside the perimeter of the drome we called a halt. Gentleman Jim had been shouting at us for moving along too slowly, having already told our young inexperienced officer to make us move faster. We had trudged along, very tired, with a number of real stragglers who were unable to keep even our slow pace. Our officer may have been one of those 'Singapore' civilian commissions, given out as hopeful protection whilst a POW. He had ordered us to move more quickly which we were unable to do — not even for Tojo himself. Gentleman Jim bawled and screamed true to style at the young officer, leaving him in no doubt what he thought of the officer's rank. The theme of Jim's admonishing, clearly indicated by his colloquialisms and gesticulations, was that Jap soldiers always did as they were told, even if it was impossible.

'You no good officer, men not do, no good officer now must die,' he said, warming to his intended ugly deeds.

Without further ado he cocked his rifle and handed it to the officer, made him kneel with face and head lowered and the rifle between his legs. He then placed the officer's forehead on the point of the barrel and indicated he should now press the trigger and become a real officer.

We were appalled at such a gutter charade, if that is what he intended.

'Would he kill himself?' — we thought not.

We hoped also that he wasn't brave enough to shoot Jim first or we may all finish up in Boot Hill even quicker than we expected. The officer had to bear his humiliation as long as the guard saw fit and we had some idea of the fear he would be feeling; anything could happen at anytime, these situations were always explosive.

For a good ten minutes the guard guffawed and sneered at the so-called lack of guts presented by the young officer. Still he did not look like pressing the trigger. Had he done so the guard would have dreamed up something for his Commandant to readily accept, then one more number would be struck from our tally. He was now ready to call a halt to his sadistic game.

'Kiotsuke Keirei!' came his order (To attention and salute/bow).

Taking back his rifle he held it towards the sky and pulled the trigger — nothing but the click of the hammer, and more belly laughs from Jim. He had either planned the whole affair or else the Japs didn't always carry a loaded rifle — and the latter didn't seem very likely.

When we arrived back at camp, he signalled that we could all go directly to our huts with no count or search. He was either avoiding any questions at the guardroom or else it was his twisted way of saying, 'That's your reward for having my fun'. It is how they often behaved. Of course, we were happy at any time to avoid a search for it meant everybody got in whatever they had picked up during the day — if anything.

For a short period we all worked in the camp, setting out fenced areas to house the sick, and we were now also allowed to build a wooden jetty out over the sea — at least, the officers were allowed to build it, not us. New trenches were dug for drains, the stream was diverted and a number of stone roads were laid throughout the camp. There were men of many trades who now quietly came out into the open with their skills. Knowing our work would bring about a slowing of the epidemic, everyone put their shoulder to the wheel and gave what energy they had left.

Deaths were now at a daily rate of twelve or more and, with many more at death's door, there were expectations of the rate growing to fifteen or even twenty a day. The burial party, always at night, was given a little candlelight to see their way to Boot Hill. The small procession was ghostlike and a permanent, nightly reminder to us all of what may be around the corner for any one of us. The bearers would stumble their way in semi-darkness over uneven rocky ground and a guard would always be in attendance, not out of respect but in case anyone was daft enough to run and be shot.

In earlier days coffins had been roughly shaped from planks of wood, then from green bamboo and now they were wrapped in anything we could find. Men deemed to be unfit were set about scratching out shallow holes for the next day's interment. At the height of the epidemic fourteen bodies had gone into one very shallow grave. On one dreadful occasion *Gunso* Mori had attended a burial when worse for drink, and the beast vomited into the grave just before the actual burial. Being physically punished is one thing but having to endure such disgusting behaviour and being unable to react is even harder to bear.

Between six and nine huts were prepared for the sick compound and numbered in order of the seriousness of the patients. No 1 was for those doomed to die, No 2 for seriously ill etc, and it was by no means difficult to make rapid progress from No 9 to No 1. Senior Doctor Bruning had to make a daily return of workers and sick to *Gunso* Mori, not to Commandant Kurishima. It seemed we had to always wait before being granted the very smallest request, so that the Japs could say it had come from them: over 250 men had died, just to save their damned faces.

When the major part of the camp work was complete we returned to the drome where there would now only be one shift each day, from dawn until 1830 hours, or whenever they decided to release us. A half-hour lunch break would be spent queueing for our rice (with weevills) and if luck held good there would be a little time left for a short rest. During the day we would have one or two very short breaks followed by excessive 'Keraja speedo' (work fast) to make up for the time we had wasted having a rest.

By the middle of July 1943, even those able to continue working outside began to show symptoms of malnutrition: tingling in the legs; burning sensations in the feet; mouth and ears numbed as though by cocaine — all symptoms of neurosis or malnutrition. Then there were those who had 'fairground balls' (unceasing itch of the scrotum), or whose testicles were swollen to an unbelievable size, or who had ringworms as large as a dinner plate. There were many more symptoms we did not even understand, yet all those with this type of problem were termed fit until unable to stand.

Our foursome was doing reasonably OK, with just one or two of the smaller problems threatening us: Bill had some numbness in his legs and signs of beriberi; Joe had a small ulcer on his calf; and I had eye troubles as my vision deteriorated and painful headaches became a daily factor. Ted, as usual, had only his permanent smile and lots of advice to give.

The four of us did our share of complaining and moaning, mainly to ease the many tensions that built up day by day, but never did we argue. If any one of us proved difficult the others came down on him immediately and automatically. It looked now as though the dysentery epidemic could be brought under control — malnutrition would probably finish off the rest of us.

By the end of July, Mori allowed a camp shop to be opened (*his* shop) where only outside workers could spend ten cents a day. First, though, the workers would have to earn a permit which Mori would allocate how and when he felt like it. The shop was stocked with ample fruit and coconuts and there was also tobacco and native cigarettes. But there was also a great deal of unrest and heightened feelings when it was seen just how easy it was to obtain the food that would so easily have saved many lives earlier on.

All our footwear was now coming to the end of its useful life and walking barefoot became the order of the day, to add to our many troubles. As we began to suffer the consequences of cut and scratched feet, we also developed tropical ulcers. A barely visible abrasion or scratch could, the very next day, begin a sore. Without thinking, it would be fingered, and within a couple of days an open ulcer half-inch across would have formed. It could, and usually did, double in size 'daily'.

The first treatment was but a wash with disinfectant and a piece of rag applied and tied with another piece. The open sore would suppurate from a red and yellow centre like a carbuncle, making walking and standing an excruciatingly painful business. Daily exertion, instead of resting, made them even bigger, yet almost as bad was the disgusting smell and attraction to flies. Some men had three, four, or even more, ulcers. When the ulcers became impossible to bear you were forced to go sick for further treatment, but not a moment before because going sick with an ulcer was a frightening experience on Haruku. The patient was laid down whilst Doctors Springer and Forbes used an ordinary sterilised spoon to clean out the ulcer which was often as large as a fifty pence piece. The doctor would always advise his 'victim' to give out his very best curses; they always obliged!

Bill was the first to show the dreaded signs of beriberi: swelling of the legs and a general numbness, and when a thumb was pressed into the leg it would leave a depression that remained for a long time. He would not be able to fight his symptoms and they were bound to worsen without nutritious foods. Joe wasn't feeling too well but was not ill enough to cause us great concern. Ted now had an itchy scrotum which was almost driving him around the bend; it was said to be a symptom of phlegra (a form of neuritis). I, with poor vision and showing the beginning of ulcers, was probably the best of a poor bunch. We were all feeling thoroughly fed up and each weighed around the eight stone mark.

It was now into August 1943. Having survived almost four months on this island, we began to wonder how long our sentence was to be. The score was 260 dead, over 800 still down with dysentery. 70 ill with general illness and 250 sick in camp huts. About 680 of us remained in bondage up at the drome, and we were the lucky ones.

Life always has its brighter moments, even on Haruku, and we were certainly ready to enjoy them. We arrived back in camp one night to see what looked like a large packing case, yet it had a seat and what might pass as a windscreen. Inside this contraption there was a centrally-placed stick. I thought it had to be some sort of medieval torture machine but it was nothing so complicated; it was supposed to represent an aeroplane cockpit and *Gunso* Mori had insisted on having it made for him to practise in. He really was as mad as a bloddy hatter! It seems that in civilian life he had worked in an aircraft factory and fancied himself as a pilot; we wished his ambition had come true — on a kamikase flight!

Gunso Mori was a man who really did defy understanding. Almost every day now, when we returned, stories of ugly incidents circulated — all instigated by Mori or his henchman, Kasiyama. A small party of prisoners who collected our few rations from the village were involved in one incident. They, of course, always had a Jap escort, though not always the same one. One guard who often escorted them was 'Bowser Bill' (Toyoda). He was a nasty type, as cruel as they come, and his usual job was to be in charge of the water cart. On this particular day he accused the RAF sergeant in charge of our party of stealing and bartering with the natives for food. The accusation was totally unfounded, nevertheless the sergeant was put on show outside the camp guardroom with his hands tied behind his back. Then the alleged ill-gotten gain (one dried fish) was tied into his mouth and there he had to stand in the fierce tropical heat in full view of everyone. During the long heat of that day hordes of flies swarmed around the fish, having a feast not only of fish but also of his flesh. This most sadistic form of torture, that can drive a man out of his senses, was enjoyed by all our captors. Needless to say we found it revolting.

On another occasion Mori decided to use his bamboo (his second nickname was 'Bamboo Mori') to beat a prisoner until it smashed into slivers on the man's back. Then a little later, emphasising his unpredictability, Mori attacked one of his own men. He fired shots through the door of a Jap hut at the very spot where this particular Jap should have been. Had he not been missing, which is what Mori suspected, he would have been murdered in his own bed. We didn't find it much fun living with this sort of unfamiliar action, never knowing which day you may be a victim, and it was not surprising that men walked around in an almost permanent state of tension. Our *Tenko* was on parade at the time Mori, having spotted the missing Jap, came ambling past wearing only a jock strap, his revolver in his hand and a drunken grin spread all over his ugly face. There really were times when it was difficult not to laugh at some of his antics.

September came and the small miracle of clothing, a pair of Dutch green shorts, was issued to outside workers only; some even managed a tunic. Otherwise September followed roughly the same pattern as those months before it.

October 1943 saw a large party of about 1,000 Dutch prisoners arrive on Haruku from Amahai (Ceram). Their arrival neither helped nor hindered our survival; on the one hand they helped a great deal labour-wise, but on the other hand we were not given any extra rations of rice for them, meaning an even more serious cut in rations. When the Dutch first arrived they were kept separate from us but later they joined us in camp. Deaths had now reached more than 300, over 1,000 were 'hospitalised', leaving approximately 760 working in one capacity or another.

> 'I shall give tongue for those who cannot speak
> But who, 'forever England' lie afar
> Our honoured dead, each special and unique
> Who turned their mortal dust into a star
> Of these then hear the tale and learn their worth
> For higher honoured have you none on earth.'
>
> Jim Hacobin (Fepow)

Among the workers I doubt if there were more than a hundred who were lucky enough to call themselves fit from our original total of 2,060. Most were now under so-called 'treatment' for ulcers, failing eyesight, painful feet and other limbs or one of many other symptoms of malnutrition.

Our little combine continued to struggle to the drome but not without our problems and aggravations. Bill was now being seriously bothered and incapacitated by his beriberi, and now dragged his feet in the ominous flip flop manner. Joe was having nasty stomach troubles yet was trying so hard to grin and bear it —

that was young Joe's style. Even Ted was now struggling a little, with no outward sign of disease yet but with a total lack of stamina that was pulling him down. When we could manage it, we worked him on filling our sacks rather than carrying the load. I was still OK except for my eyes, which were beginning to worry me; I could no longer stand the glare from the coral rocks. If my sight continued to deteriorate at the same alarming rate, I would be blind before the year was out, as others were, and would soon leave for Java. On top of that I had what the doctor called corneal ulcers, which suppurated causing a small scab on my eyeballs. It was a constant worry when my eyes wept onto my face and I was plagued with blowflies which almost drove me insane. Nevertheless we were as good as most, better than many and we did have each other, at least for the time being.

The Japs had now accepted that unless we were given proper tools, manpower would run out before their project neared completion. Who would explain to 'old nitty whiskers' or 'the old goat' (both suitable descriptions for Major Anami) the reasons for their failure? I believe that Anami, who had a long scraggy beard, was the senior Jap on the island of Haruku.

From a nearby island the Japs had collected explosive charges which included a number of small bombs, most likely their 125-pounders, for blasting purposes. Instead of our chiselling away at the coral rock with 6-12″ chisels, we were now digging out suitable holes for the charges or the bombs. It was a most welcome change for it allowed us to sit or lay on the ground as we worked, considerably easing our work load. When we found a soft seam we kept quiet and played it for all we were worth. This change of practice did, however, bring yet another scare — that of being blown sky high. The soldiers in charge were not too skilled in demolition work, often detonating before we were all clear: there were times we swore this was done on purpose.

Each day, if we looked for it, there would be some kind of interesting diversion, and very often a tough character called Lofty was the centre of it. If there were any slappings you could bet Lofty was always the victim. He was arrogant and the Japs didn't care too much for him; they could always be assured the feeling was mutual as far as Lofty was concerned. If a guard upset Lofty he would return the compliment at the first opportunity.

On this particular day an explosion was triggered off and our friend Lofty got off to a slow start when a piece of coral hit him on the head — not uncommon. Typically, he saw the possibility of some gain from the small bleeding wound on his hard nut. He thought if he showed the guard he was bleeding then he would be on a good thing having done it in the 'Emperor's' employment. Approaching the guard, Lofty asked for a *roko* (cigarette) but he came unstuck and received the lighted cigarette on his nearest leg. Like others before him he got the cigarette and a large grin. It was a wonder this lad Lofty didn't have a go at the guard then and there, for his face told a fearsome story of hate and a promise that one day he would repay with massive interest. We had to quickly turn away for fear of bursting out in laughter.

By the middle of October 1943 we had our first real problem in the combine in that Bill's beriberi had caught up with him and he also had the beginnings of dysentery. I always had an awful feeling, almost a premonition about Bill, and it greatly saddened me for it was one of doom. He now had no option but to stay back one morning and attend the sick parade where he was at once put into hut No 2. We were now down to three.

Each night we took it in turns to sit a while with Bill, giving him any drome news and hopefully maintaining his interest in the outside world, as nasty as it was. If we managed to scrounge anything to eat then Bill got more than his share. The three of us felt, though no one would say or voice an opinion, that Bill was but the first nail in our mutual coffin.

November 1943 saw the working parties much depleted, so a further purge was made by Blood and Slime in which two hundred men were taken from the sick huts and paraded. An elderly Dutchman in one hut suffering from beriberi was felled by Mori's famous bamboo because he had not come onto the parade. The orderly who came forward to assist the old chap was similarly treated for interfering. From now on, any time the drome quota was not reached, Mori would tear around the camp swinging his bamboo in one hand whilst he rode a cycle with the other. He was an awesome sight as he raced down the sloping camp ground felling anyone who stood in his way, believing that the more intolerable he made camp life the more likely he would be to drive the sick out and back to the drome. Most of those he succeeded in driving out would return in a day or two more sick than ever — often it became the difference between life and death for the unfortunates.

Thankfully we were seeing some slight improvement in our living conditions; it was then that a Jap 'doctor' decided it was time to pay us a visit.

He was classic and had all the answers, no bother:

'It's your own fault, all you need do is kill the flies and cut your finger nails,' was his diagnosis!

He then paraded our officers to expound his theory and cure all, after which he left, never to be seen again. That was the measure of his interest — not a good omen.

On 16th November 1943 a party of 150 so-called 'fit' men were taken to Ambon island, travelling across the water in a native *prauw* (boat). At the same time 650 sick men were being prepared for a return to Java via Ambon. Bill and Pat McGrogan would be on that draft, as would another friend, Martin Oldfield, who was almost blind. No doubt they would all be very apprehensive about the sea journey with their recent trip still fresh in their memories. In many cases these men were only rested in Java until such time as they were able to stand on their own two feet again. Then they were once more on the high seas — God help them — to Singapore, Sumatra or Japan. Not everyone would make it. Unfortunately, many moved from the troubles of Haruku into equally miserable and squalid surroundings.

Our death toll had now reached 363 which we hoped was a peak. The worst of our sick were dumped into the hold of their ship for most of them to die *en route* to Java. Somewhere along the route, I suspect at Ambon, Bill became separated from the others. Pat and Martin were lucky not to be transferred to the other ship at Ambon, for that ship was the *Suez Maru* which was sunk by an Allied submarine between Macassar (Celebes) and Java on 29th November 1943. No prisoners survived: the few prisoners who had survived the torpedo attack were machine-gunned in the water by a small Jap escort vessel. All but two of the Japs on board (most were wounded soldiers) were believed to have also drowned. The two Japs rumoured to have survived were said to be camp guards who later turned up at Haruku dressed in new clothing.

I was now left to wonder whether that feeling of doom about Bill had now become a reality. Luckily, Pat and Martin on the other ship left Ambon on 14th

November 1943, and arrived safely at Tandjoeng Perak, Sourabaya, on 19th December 1943. From there they entrained to Batavia. arriving on 21st December in time to hang up their dirty old shorts for Christmas.

At Haruku every effort was still being made to rebuild the camp. It had come too late for many, but it would help those still with some hope of survival. Roads were completed with stones from the river — no longer would it be necessary to walk in bare feet over muddy and fouled ground. Gardens were made, though none of the produce came our way except vegetable tops which were always acceptable. Our captors gave us nothing but a hard time, grinding us further and further into the dust.

One of the most hated tasks that befell us after a trying and difficult day at the drome was stone collecting. Arriving back at camp, dead beat and desperate for rest, a sniggering guard would be waiting to meet us at the gate.

'Lecas, alle men, yasumae nai,' (Quickly, all men, no rest) would be his mocking cry.

We then had to trek up and down to the river bed in our bare feet to gather stones. As we carried them past a guard he would look to see if they were large enough for his liking. Should they not be, then we usually received a hefty swipe, and were taken back to lift the heaviest he could find before being sent on our way again — often at the double. We would be kept there until the guard saw fit to release us and I remember one of these gatherings brought about my most severe depression — that was until things got worse.

We were now allowed a few small fires in the huts and with them a new challenge was born for ingenious minds — what could we do with a fire? The scroungers came into their own, as they were sent off to find, beg, borrow or steal tools with which to cook: a tin in which to fry or bake, or a piece of tin spiked with some sharp instrument to be used as a grater. Bits of wood, and above all coconut oil which would have to be obtained from the natives, became like liquid gold. The Dutch showed us how to make a jungle Ronson to light our fires which proved to be indispensable. Our steamed rice ration with grated coconut and coconut milk, together with grated roots of God knows what, all went into a cake mixture which could be baked in a tin. Not many men were capable or interested health-wise to take advantage of this cooking, so the baker would often trade and on odd occasions he would raffle or auction a small cake for cash.

With permission from an attendant guard we were now allowed to wash in the sea — indeed we were becoming very privileged people. The very first chap that ran into the sea, however, was shot at (over the head); apparently no one had bothered to tell the guard it was OK. Also, we at last received our second small piece of soap, and with careful use I gave myself a good clean up — it was sheer ecstasy! When it next rained we again stood under the eaves of the hut, pushing and shoving for the best positions, and repeated this until the soap was all gone.

Everything except our health, strength and state of mind showed some improvement. Many had by now reached that point of no return, but little did we know that the future held much more to endure and overcome before we would get back home.

> Lord, thou hast given me a cell
> Herein to dwell
> A little hut with all its filth

Lord, help me be determined
To live, in spite
Of this man-made hell

Lord, thou has put me to the test
I shall do my very best
To live in this hell
You have asked me to dwell
Lord, we all feel the pain
Do not let it happen again

Anon.

At about this time Doctor Springer was forced to carry out an operation on a perforated stomach ulcer. A makeshift theatre was set up in one of the huts and, ably assisted by Dr Bruning and Dr Phelps, the operation was successfully completed.

Then the calm was broken once more. Another epidemic broke out, not so much a killer as very painful and thoroughly demoralising — tropical ulcers. With no footwear, except for those who had managed to make wooden clompers out of a flat piece of wood and a single cloth strap across the toes, the drome was very rough going and the skin was regularly broken. Lack of nutrition continued, and our resistance became even lower as the ulcers developed and became a very serious matter. The greatest of all dangers came from the strong possibility of gangrene developing. There were no available medicines, only the ingenious concoctions that our doctors kept producing. In the worst cases maggots were deliberately placed in the wound before it was covered — the maggots would clean out the wound very successfully and would then be removed. Almost all outside workers could be seen sporting old pieces of rag around their legs, covering one or two ulcers of varying sizes.

The three of us plodded on into late December 1943 amid strong reports of air raids on Ambon Town. All three of us were now under the weather and had reached the stage when men talked continually of home and families, dwelling on whether we would see them again. For so long we had agreed not to do that for it was depressive and sapped morale. We could never find anything that gave us any comfort or belief that we would ever return. A refusal to be beaten — a bulldog spirit if you like — was what kept most of us going in adversity. We would think of pigs like Kasiyama who would say in all seriousness:

'You should let your friends die. They are sick and of no use, and it will make things easier for you.'

Refusing to satisfy him was encouragement enough.

Joe was getting much worse and could only make the drome with the help of Ted and me. Ted and I were also passing through a depression stage when more trouble came upon us in the shape of American bombers — Liberators. We felt they were more likely to kill us than liberate us. They came in at midday from roughly 2,000 feet and appeared to be looking for the Jap barracks. We were doing our usual blasting when they were first sighted like silver bullets in line with the barracks and the airstrip.

There was no cover at all except for the cylindrical holes we were digging and they would be no more than 1'6" at the most. If we dived into a hole we would stand upright at about chest height ready to be decapitated by any anti-personnel bombs that may be dropped. That way there would have been no tomorrows to worry about, but self preservation always wins through. The alternative was to flee as fast as our legs would carry us into the nearby undergrowth and play the ostrich. Whichever way we chose, you could safely bet that the guards were there first. They were never so brave when unsure of their situation and lacking a clear target to kill.

Our working party included many sick people forced out by Mori, and we were fortunate to have only four casualties, two of whom were injured seriously. All the injured were RAF lads, one of whom later died due to the delay in receiving treatment. The others suffered badly with aggravated shock even after their wounds healed. Chest wounds, legs, thighs and posteria suggested that anti-personnel bombs had been used. At times like that it was with mixed feelings that we welcomed our Yankee 'friends'; to see them approach was satisfying and to some extent morale-boosting; to be under their bombs was to curse them; to have your friends killed by their submarines or aircraft was to hate them, be it only for a fleeting moment; then to watch them return to the 'freedom' of their base was to envy them; knowing that one day they would be back to free us with all that attendant risk, was to admire and respect them. Whatever your thoughts on their visits, you could never manage to ignore them.

The native *kampong* had been most unlucky having 200 killed or injured and receiving no help whatsoever from the Japs. Our Dr Bruning sought permission to take a number of our doctors in to help the native casualties and consent was given — but three days later when most were in a really dreadful state. Doctors Springer, Phelps and Forbes went into the village and spent the best part of a day treating the injured. This included one amputation, using supplies provided by the Japs from a source they could never locate for us. Even then, the Japs still refused to allow our doctors a follow-up visit; no doubt the enemy had no wish for any friendship to develop between the natives and oursleves. A working party of prisoners was, however, allowed into the village to help them out, for their living quarters had been almost obliterated and the village was now almost non-existent: it appeared to us that the Liberators had mistaken the *kampong* for the Japanese barracks — such a shame. In the village we saw plentiful supplies of fruit, whilst in camp lads were dying for the need of it. We did benefit from that, though, as the natives allowed us to loot.

By mid-December 1943 a yeast had been prepared by our own Doctor Audus. It was made from rice washings and a kedala milk which came from beans. The stones needed to grind the rice and beans were hewn from a solid rock by an elderly Dutch stonemason. Issues of the yeast were made at the rate of 100cc to all sick men, and 300cc to those with beriberi — there is no doubt that the yeast went a long way towards saving, or at least prolonging, life.

New Year 1944 brought us very little luck. Joe could no longer make the drome, and it was a very sad time for me as I watched my best friend rapidly deteriorating, suffering from both dysentery and beriberi. Our little combine was now down to two. I have no doubt both Ted and I wondered who was next but no word was spoken. The two of us worked together on the *tanga*'s whenever we could manage it, sometimes overlooked by a none-too-friendly guard we knew as the 'Black Bastard'. I'm not too sure of this gentleman's name and I could be wrong about the nickname. However, his description will be recognisable by many of my friends. He was an elderly *gunso* and a drug addict who inhaled his drug as though it were snuff. He was often in charge of the fuel and bomb dumps and he was as explosive as the materials he cared for — another one to avoid at all times.

Occasionally we would be lucky enough to join a party going into the nearby Jap aircrew barracks, which was a slightly more civilised place. Here, there was a *gunso* who actually asked if we wished to take shelter from the heavy rains. At other times he would send some beautiful thick soup, or was it the nectar of the Gods? The taste was the same, I'm sure. He was like any normal fellow, and we thought he would have no friends of his own kind if they were aware of his great weakness of being kind.

It was at these barracks that I unconsciously raised at least one good laugh back in camp. I was working on a good number in ablutions when I picked up a floorcloth and noticed it was a nice piece of crepe de Chine. The material was rather dirty with use but I could spot anything useful; by now I had already knocked off a couple of small pieces of soap and could see the potential of nice clean material. I imagined it was large enough to make a useful covering of my more personal parts when my shorts gave up on me. Now I only had to get it clean, washed and dried ready to take back to camp.

Rubbing as much of their soap as I could into it I used it to wash all the wash basins etc, constantly wringing it out until it was spotless. The sun later dried it out at the back of the building. If questioned there was no problem as I was 'just washing out my floorcloth ready for the next day': even taking this old cloth out could be seen as thieving if they felt that way, so one could not afford to be careless. It may be difficult to believe anyone had to go to such limits for an old piece of rag, but remember we were allowed nothing unless it was given by a guard, and even that could be fateful.

Back in camp, using my RAF housewife (needle and cottons) which was my only remaining possession, I cut and roughly shaped the material into the briefest of shorts, then stitched it all together and quietly slipped into the soft and clean crepe de Chine to try them on. I honestly thought nothing of the consequences that might follow. Perhaps I was very naive for I hadn't gone more than a few yards in the hut before it started. I suspect that someone like my old friend Charlie Mantle, or else Cunningham, both off the HMS *Electra*, started it. Yes, it was the most embarrassing moment, possibly in my life, and those wolf calls still ring in my ears. I cannot remember where I dumped those shorts but I did it quickly after everyone had had a damned good laugh — which wasn't a bad thing. How I ever managed to lift my head again as word spread I shall never know. To this day old Charlie will still not admit anything. Such was life on Haruku, that we never knew where the next laugh might come from, but on that day it was my privilege. Due to those shorts, I shall always remember the small kindness at that barracks and the one *gunso*. But as sometimes happens, a few of the more self-centred ones amongst us abused the well-intentioned guards and those barracks soon became as harsh as anywhere else on the island.

Our combine of two continued the regular trips to the drome until well into the New Year of 1944. Then my next calamity struck and it happened at the most depressed period of my stay on Haruku. We had only just finished blasting some of the rock surface and it was about time to clear up the resultant debris and carry it away. After this last explosion there was a large piece of rock not yet freed at its base. I would need to chisel at it before it could be moved — often a hard slow job with a two-pound hammer. At the end of the day this pig of a guard I knew as 'Flatface' stood watching me clear the loose stuff from around the base of the really large boulder. When I had finished he ambled over showing all the cocky signs I should have recognised and been warned by — he was so obviously looking for trouble with a capital 'T'. First came the usual stare and sneers, and the crude grunting, then:

'Kurra. Kono Yaro' followed by 'Ingris, tida bagus . . . grunt . . . grunt . . . tida abis.' (English no good — not finished.)

At the same time he gesticulated that I should move the large rcock. I was to move it alone with no other help. For the very first time in my life I couldn't have cared less what he wanted or how he intended to get it done — I had reached the end, I thought.

'Wakara nai,' (Understand not) I said quite indifferently.

He screamed like some caged animal just let loose on its prey, so with more wisdom I tried English-style logic on him, showing where it was fastened at its base, then I said:

'Sato orang tida' (One man, no) followed by 'Banya orang mari sine OK?' (More men, come here, OK?)

My blood was reaching danger point and my mental state total confusion — I was at my wits end. I had reached that point when I just didn't care about living. I had endured enough and wanted no more. Threatening and bawling, upset by my reactions, Flatface replied:

'Tida, satu orang, keraja, lecas.' (No, one man, work, fast.)

I made an effort and pushed and made every reasonable sign of gracious defeat as I tried to indicate again that I wanted no trouble, only a logical conclusion to something I couldn't do. Then came the first kick on the shin that carried my new ulcer; it was the most excruciating pain I had ever felt or have ever felt since and I did the one thing he wanted — I lost my temper.

Everyone has a breaking point and I had reached mine. I turned sharply towards him in no uncertain manner, hiding none of my emotions, and told him what to do and where to go. One has to be in such a position to appreciate the very thin line between being brave and downright stupid as I was. The former often won medals unexpectedly, the other often brought havoc or even death.

'Shift it your ******* self!' I screamed.

My face must have said the rest as I turned to walk away.

Voices just outside of my senses would have been warning me to stop and shut up; I never heard them nor saw the shocked faces of my friends. Perhaps I wanted someone else to finish that difficult time for me — it was something I would never know as one could not account for such happenings. The leering stance of Flatface must have been a sight to behold as he snarled:

'Apa birchara?' (What say?) then 'Bitchara, sama, sama.) (Say, same again.)

Realising something was going badly wrong I tried to think my way out of the mess I had created. I repeated the same, only in a more conciliatory manner. He was not impressed.

'Tida, sama sama,' (Not the same) he further shouted, before landing me one hell of a clout in the face with his clenched fist. He followed up on alternate sides as fast as he was able. His technique, well-practised, sent me reeling from left to right as he went into his 'slapping' action. This time it didn't seem to hurt as much as on previous occasions — I seemed to have a mental block against the physical pain.

In retrospect I don't honestly think I would have cared if he had put me away for good. He was still persisting that I shift the rock and as I remained upright he started again:

'Bitchara, sama sama, kono yaro.' (Say same again, stupid.)

I knew he wasn't finished with me yet so I gave him a repeat with even more venom applied. It wasn't too difficult, as either way I was going to pay for my indiscretion. I shall never forget the snarls, the fierce and hideous appearance of the wild animal that may have looked like man, yet was something more primeval. I made a determined effort to remain upright as I knew I must do, until with one final swing of his rifle butt, he turned and stalked away. His sadism was now satisfied and his bloody face saved — Ted and others came quickly to the assistance of a much wiser young man.

The New Year continued to be unfortunate and it looked as though our essential search and loot for food would bring serious trouble. A number of Dutch and British had visited a nearby plantation belonging to the natives; we believed that as long as the visits were not abused the natives would turn a blind eye in return for the help received after the bombing. As always, and the British are no exception, there are those who will greedily grab and take whatever they can lay hands on.

During one midday break as we sat struggling with our rice and watery tea, an Indonesian appeared on the scene. He was very irate, and the Dutch lads told us that he owned the plantation. Apparently he knew nothing about the lads helping themselves with any form of approval. Thankfully our guard had wandered off, no doubt to sit with his friends, otherwise the Indonesian could well have approached him first — it looked as though he was of the minority who would be much closer to the enemy than others.

The man shouted for immediate payment of the stolen fruit he had seen the last raiders take before returning to our party. The Dutch lads did their best to placate him. It was important at all costs to hang on to whatever food they had, but he would have none of it. He was obviously asking for money and threatening to go to the guard which would have been catastrophic. He was asking for ten guilders, no small sum in our circumstances, and, in a panic, one of the Dutchmen paid — not many Britishers had money. Still not satisfied, he wanted more and refused to go until someone gave him a watch or a ring — the beginning of blackmail. He was no friend. Some of our lads wanted to threaten or punch him there and then whilst others were at panic stations. The latter were wise to be concerned as Tojo was expected back at any time and none of us wanted *his* trouble, so the native was given what he demanded by someone. So now another plantation was out of bounds; they were few and small and soon there would be nowhere left, to search, except the wild undergrowth.

Some time in November 1943 another similar incident occurred, only this time involving an Indonesian woman who gave fruit to some of the lads on the drome. They were seen by one of the guards as the woman sped back into the jungle. Four or five lads were tackled by the guard and all but one admitted involvement — anyone would think a ghastly crime had been committed. It was usually better to admit guilt and take whatever followed, for their judgement would already be made. They had to kneel on the sharp and rocky ground without any form of food and drink until they returned to camp some five hours later. Kneeling on the ground for long periods is sufficient torture on that terrain — where by lifting one knee the pain on the other was doubled — without the added pain of the tropical heat. The fifth man did not confess and we know him to be innocent yet he was handed over to the camp guards upon our return. With great pleasure they found him guilty and advised Mori, who was most pleased, to teach him a sharp lesson not to lie. He had to take a beating like a man — an innocent one but no one cared.

In 1984 I spoke with a friend, a fellow Ex-Pow who had just returned from a visit to Haruku where he had met the people of the village. The headman of the village of Palao, son of the wartime headman, told how his father had been beheaded by the Japs for giving food to prisoners.

During January and February, Joe's condition rapidly worsened, but there was little we could do for him except visit him in Hut No 1, when permitted. The orderly had told Ted that Joe was in a bad way; he had struggled along outside until he no longer had the strength left to fight. What a brutal situation when a lad fights to stay alive then no longer has the resources when he finally needs them. But each of us had to make his own decisions, just as Joe had.

It was 30th March 1944, a day I shall always remember. I staggered back into camp to be told, I think by Dick Keefe:

'Jim, Joe Parker has died.'

I had not believed I was capable of crying over one more death having lived with it for over a year but this wasn't just another death, it was Joe, my best friend. Something inside of me died with Joe that day, as though I could no longer believe in the Christian teachings I had received. I felt I had come face to face with reality and was seeing a vicious and cruel world for what it really was. For a moment I must have wondered if this is how Ted would feel about me if I was next. I cried shamelessly over Joe. He was the fifth 242 Squadron lad to die out there on Haruku; Sergeant Peake and Jock Cummins had only recently gone to a more restful and peaceful place. Now two of our combine were left — two down and two to go.

The camp building had gone on through February and new huts were built for Mori and Kasiyama in even more prominent positions. During these activities Mori was in a kinder mood, almost civilised, giving out tickets to be used in his shop. On other occasions Mori would sit up on our steamless steam roller and have a team of prisoners pull him along; it was difficult to know which fantasy role he was playing on that occasion!

During March and April 1944, small parties, mostly Dutch, left Palao camp on Haruku. One British party accompanied the Dutch and among them was my home-town friend, Ron Taylor. Their destination on the island of Ambon was the camp at Liang. Our next casualty was another friend, Geoff Lee, who, when being given instructions by Kasiyama, made a snide remark which Tokyo Taff overheard. He pulled Geoff out and gave him a beating which broke Geoff's forearm. However, all was not bad luck for Geoff, as the the next day he was seen on light duties as a rice server, for a mere smashed forearm! After all, if he had been unlucky he could have ended up as a left-handed fly catcher!

During the last couple of months there had been rumours that a truce had been signed or that the war was actually over. In the past we had talked so many times of the most crucial days yet to come, particularly the day when the Japs were beaten or, even worse, when they faced defeat in the area where we were imprisoned. What would happen to us? Was our present effort to stay alive worth the trouble? Not a pleasant subject, but one never far from the mind which would never go away. The strongest possibility was our immediate disposal, and the variety of methods that could be used were endless, inoculation or massacre being the favourite opinions. Indeed, the latter is exactly what happened to some Australians we had left behind on Ambon when setting off for Java.

At about this time we were told that the Japs were to give injections to about thirty of us. Our doctors warned the men not to make a fuss as they had a pre-determined plan. Apparently the doctors believed this was an experimental solution the Japs wished to try out for the benefit of their Military. If at the time there were any doubters of the Japs' reasons for this act, they will now be aware that much worse practices were carried out on prisoners of war in Mongolia.

Our own doctors were giving the injections with a guard in attendance. The doctor dabbed the arm with his cotton wool and picked the flesh up with his left hand still holding the cotton wool pad. The solution went straight into the cotton wool pad as the victim blinked his eyes with the pain he never felt. The lads knew that nothing had penetrated their skin. No more injections were called for.

Ted remained in reasonable shape, and my own vision slightly improved as I managed to get a few jobs in shady spots, and we pressed on as the months crawled past. A party of 150 mainly 'stretcher' cases together with Flying Officer Jordan, were gathered in the open at about noon and in the pouring rain. Clothing and any possessions except for those men wore were taken from them. They were told they would receive new clothing when they reached Java, if they ever did. Those who eventually made it to Java did so some time during August 1944.

This 150-strong party was taken to the ferry point, with stretcher cases on lorries, whilst the remaining sick people were force-marched the four miles. When the ferry was reached the very small native boat was found to hold only fifty, including the stretcher cases. The remaining one hundred sick men were kept outside in the ceaseless rains, when shelter could easily have been found. That same evening at about 8pm the hundred, still soaked to the skin in the cold night air, were told:

'No ship, all sick people walk back to camp.'

When they eventually arrived back at camp our CO attempted to recover their clothes and belongings. The only answer Squadron Leader Pitts received was:

'No, men go again soon.'

They left again some days later by which time the Jap transport to Java had left. With no ship available the sick men, now in Ambon, were put to work on road building and airstrip work. Apparently their illnesses were mysteriously cured. This hundred or so eventually reached Java on 3rd September 1944, probably on the *Taian Maru*.

Back on Haruku the fly-catching continued, and everyone who could lift an arm had to aim for a target of three hundred a day each! The day's catch had to be presented at the evening *Tenko*: not enough flies to satisfy Mori or Kasiyama meant even less rice or none at all. The crazy thing was that we repeatedly asked for permission to get rid of the breeding grounds — the stagnant pools around the camp — but that request was always refused; their Doctor had said we must catch flies and that was that! No co-peration was ever forthcoming; it seemed it was all part of a planned campaign to wear us down and injure our health. A typical Jap attitude was:

'If a Nippon animal in the fields cannot work (for the Emperor, son of Heaven) then it is useless — prisoners are the same.'

Our medical staff had now produced a paste made up of Jap tooth powder, chalk and coconut oil plus another ingredient which caused it to harden until fairly stiff. This paste was spread over a cleansed ulcer which was then covered and left while the paste hardened and protected the soft fleshy wound. It was yet another self-help introduction into the now serious ulcer epidemic. Before the paste could be applied a rather nasty treatment had to be endured, one which was only acceptable as a very last resort. The worst of the ulcer was cut away and drained about the perimeter to be rid of the stagnant blood. The only antiseptic available was a boric acid powder and there were no anaesthetics of any sort. This operation that many were compelled to undergo was most distressing and some had the treatment more than once. No wonder men in their unhealthy condition found survival rather difficult.

From time to time we enjoyed a good belly laugh. Charlie Mantle, leading stoker and a real character, always seemed to be around at those times. He was walking through camp one day with Tubby Hocking, a Welshman from 242 Squadron, when Charlie caused quite a commotion. He and Tubby were troubled with badly failing eyesight and ulcers, which is why they were working in camp, building huts. Charlie, typically, had donned a pair of very bright yellow pyjamas given to him by a Dutchman who was dying. Being the joker that he was he couldn't wait to show them off and give us all a laugh. Unfortunately for Charles, he bumped into Blood (Mori) who couldn't see the funny side — after all why should a prisoner ever laugh? Or maybe he was jealous of never having owned such a nice bright pair of pyjamas!

At any other time it was about the only level of humour he would have responded to. That day, however, he called for Slime (Kasiyama) who was in charge of the camp working party and gave him a really good dressing down and a kick up the backside (literally) in front of the lads. No doubt the lads enjoyed that but they had to suffer the backlash for the rest of the day: Kasiyama had 'lost face'. Mori ordered Charlie and Bill into a bamboo cage with these parting words:

'Be happy until you die.'

He didn't actually mean them to die that day; it was simply the way he had with words.

For the next few days friends rallied around. Mori had left no guard on the two men as he was only interested in them having an uncomfortable time. Their friends passed bits of rice through the bamboo or anything they could scrounge outside or from the cookhouse where matloes worked — they always looked after their own. After a few days they were released and looked no worse for their discomfort. It was just a pity those pyjamas were now soiled and rather dirty!

Not long afterwards Blood had another brainstorm. In his usual drunken fashion after much sake or native drink, he put in an appearance at the guardroom in the early hours of the morning. He was a big man for a Jap, with wide shoulders and a barrel chest; the build and the strength of a wrestler. When he was drunk, even his own people did their best to avoid him — I thought he was a psychopath! On this occasion he found his guards were not alert, so for the rest of the night he made them trot up and down the river carrying stones. After bringing them to the camp, where they would have been useful to us, he made them return every one to the river bed. When tired of this exercise he made them all change into full battle dress and remain on duty until daylight. The whole incident was seen by our senior NCO's who were in the hut opposite the guardroom; many lads would have sacrificed much-needed sleep to have witnessed such a pleasing sight.

Before we left Haruku, there was yet another incident I can recall, though not in its entirety. It was claimed that two guards connected in some way with their medical staff had gone absent without leave. Then the jungle radio told us that they had been caught on the island of Ceram. The rumour gained in strength and was said to have originated from Kasiyama — I believe it was authentic. The hearsay was that the Jap commandant made the escapees build their own cage about five feet by six — that does follow a known practice. Then the two guards were forced into their cage and each was given a revolver and one bullet. They were then invited to shoot themselves as punishment for their transgression. After two or three days it was said one had shot himself, but the other refused to do so. The second guard, a man we knew as 'Tojo the Bastard', was said to have been freed and put solely on camp duties. That he did come into camp was factual for he was known to give the working parties hell. It was difficult to understand why he should have got off so lightly, unless they thought the first was mad for having shot himself. But then, it always was a total waste of time trying to understand their reasoning for anything.

Work in camp and on the drome followed its usual style until July 1944 when the camp strength was down to about 1,400, which *included* the Amahai 1,000. The airstrip was not quite finished though it was useable. For some reason our captors decided to clear the camp of prisoners. We were to be moved to various existing camps on the nearby island of Ambon. It was said that they wanted us all on Ambon ready to be shipped back to Java or wherever else they had in mind. From Haruku, parties of 100 to 500 were moved out, including the sick, and usually in small boats. I left on 13th July 1944, and finished up in the Liang camp. Some had gone to other camps such as Romah Tiga, Wyjami and possibly Paso.

A small party of about a hundred was left behind on Haruku to complete the rebuilding programme; they would follow us later. The camp at Palao (Haruku) had been transformed from an unbelievable filthy hovel into the best camp the Japs had on those islands, and it had cost us very dearly; behind us were the bodies of 415 men who had been sentenced to their early graves, and many more would be following them before Java was reached. The evidence of Japanese indifference and inhuman treatment of others was left behind on Haruku, to be long-remembered by their friends.

After the war, the War Graves Commission exhumed the bodies from Haruku and buried them with their Ambon friends in the new cemetery on Ambon Island. Perhaps one day the 'guilty' Japanese will emulate the actions of our own Paddy McQuade, the Irish orderly at Haruku, and learn that:

> The genuine dignity of man
> Is in his own self-discipline
> Nothing whatever to do with
> His status or his authority.

8. SOME DO GET BACK

I left Haruku with about a hundred others in a small boat travelling westwards to the camp of Liang at the northern tip of Ambonia. Speaking with friends who had reached Liang some weeks earlier, I found them to be rather disturbed at the manner in which the camp was being disciplined. It seemed that in addition to being subjected to the very harsh rule of our enemy, they also had to be most careful not to fall foul of their own continued army rules and punishments; so many prisoners at Liang carried an additional burden, which was most difficult to bear. A good friend told me:

'Believe me, Jim, I was late on parade (*Tenko*) one morning and expected to be sorted out by the Japs. Instead I was told that I was on a charge and to report to the British CO later. I was sentenced to run up and down the camp carrying a log in my arms. I had enough trouble carrying my bloody self never mind his log, so I refused, to be told that I risked a court martial when I returned home — if I ever did.

At Haruku our CO had used a different and much more sensitive approach. He and his fellow officers considered rightly that the circumstances were not in accordance with the Geneva Convention, therefore he felt they had to earn respect. Most of them did and that was to the benefit of us all. Here at Liang all ranks were still being recognised and duties being performed accordingly: the officers and NCO's ran the inside of the camp; the Japs ran the outside, and the inside when they saw fit to do so. Consequently the inmates, somewhere between the two layers of authority, were subjected to discipline during every waking moment, whereas we had been able to gain the maximum relaxation once back in camp at night.

We were told of two men who had been sentenced to jail (within Liang camp) for stealing rice from their own store — a jail within a jail! No matter how despicable a prisoner's action there could never be a satisfactory excuse or reason for inflicting further punishment on those already carrying a very heavy burden. Any serious misdemeanour (there were very few) which called for further punishment surely ought to have been dealt with at a later date, as we would have been dealt with at Haruku? Our presence at Liang may have helped, though some may have preferred to label us an undisciplined rabble. Any attempt to enforce their discipline upon us would have created problems. Had we been exposed to that type of discipline at Haruku, few men would have escaped death from the epidemics and the treatment we received; it was imperative that morale be kept high, always. We had needed to be one large family forever helping each other and, whilst rank and status counted for very little, respect for each other was paramount.

Not everyone was compelled to work outside whilst we were at Liang as apparently there were now more prisoners on Ambon than work to be done. Apart from one or two trips across the bay loading empty shell cases onto ships, I spent most of my working time on the airstrip. I had hoped to find extra food outside, for the food position in Liang was even worse than Haruku. There was regular bombing on Ambon Town and the drome workers needed more lives than the proverbial cat.

I was inside the camp when I experienced my first Ambon raid. Most of the bombs had fallen on the airstrip but two hit our camp. I was laying on the rocky uneven floor of the hut alongside the elderly Flight Sergeant Thompson, and we were actually lifted an inch or two by the impact of a bomb nearby. I felt lucky yet again, until some bright wag called out:

'Next time, mate, I would use a slit trench. They usually use anti-personnel bombs.' As if we didn't already know that!

I didn't appreciate the 'next time' remark either. It was not known at this time that the Allies were making progress towards us; a fact that would have been received with mixed feelings. There was a real fear of our likely demise the moment Allied troops set foot anywhere near the island.

In the meantime the Japs intended to cram prisoners into every inch of space on ships heading north-west. We were aware that more and more submarines must be patrolling and more aircraft on the lookout for any Japanese ship. It would be true to say that we were none too happy with our present situation, nor with the foreseeable future.

One pleasing feature was my meeting up with one or two more lads from the North East. The first Geordie I met was my good friend, Joe Connor, from Framwellgate Moor. The second was Bertie Lambert, a Sergeant Pilot who had flown one of the last Hurricanes out of Palembang along with Terence Kelly of 258 Squadron. Bertie lived opposite my own brother in Middlesbrough and he had attended the same school as myself; it was often such a small world even so far away.

Joe Connor was a well-known figure in Liang. Known as 'The Trader' he knew the ropes and was well-organised. He said:

'Stick with me, Jim, I'll see you OK.'

I did stick with Joe Connor and whenever he obtained any extra *makan* (food) I was often a beneficiary. The only things he didn't share were the slappings when he was caught.

I was still troubled about Ted's whereabouts. Rumour had it that he could be in a camp named Romah Tiga so it was just possible I might yet find him when we were shipped to Java. For the moment I was the last of our combine, which had been cruelly split asunder — one dead, one believed drowned, one missing and yours truly in deep despair. The odds were not very good for anyone now and many had reached a state of acceptance, often the first sign of a downward slide.

Those last few weeks on Ambon were far from pleasant, the shortage of food becoming even more acute. Soon we would be counting our grains of rice. The guards were also becoming tetchy and on some occasions were almost trigger happy, and nervous; something obviously troubled them deeply which worried us. Something was going on and not knowing what was more disturbing to the nervous system than standing on the edge of a volcano — or so it felt to us at the time. It seemed that news was filtering through to the guards that their blessed Nippon was not, after all, invincible.

At night we would drop off to sleep hungry and waken to that same hunger —
cracks began to appear in our resistance. Everything now began to look hopeless,
even to the strongest of men. The spirit and dignity we had held on to so jealously
was showing signs of breaking up, and that would be fatal. It was noticeable that
those being punished no longer seemed concerned; there was that feeling of
impunity I had experienced for a moment at Haruku with Flatface. My head
constantly pained me until I accepted it as a way of life, and I still do, forty years
later. Even the abundant sarcastic humour changed to nastiness and selfishness,
finishing in arguments, fights and even distrust between friends. The tension and
despair mingled with fear as life appeared to be winding itself up into a frenzy. The
atmosphere was electric and in some ways more frightening than all the deaths on
Haruku — again it was that fear of the unknown. If we didn't get off this island
soon there would only be the one journey left to make — into the Liang Boot Hill.
No one enjoyed the thought of another sea journey but the majority thought that
if we were caught in an island invasion we would doubtless be eliminated, whereas
if we reached Java, or even Singapore, we would have the possible safety of large
numbers.

The air attacks continued on Ambon Town and we saw for the first time a new
fighter-bomber, the twin fuselage Lockheed Lightning. They suddenly arrived
without any warning from over a hill strafing everything in front of them, as we
headed full bore for the jungle, again playing the ostrich game of heads down in
any sizeable depression. When all went quiet we braves ventured out, stood back
and stared with incredulity at the huge oil storage not a hundred yards from our
'cover'! Life was still an endless effort to avoid death by one form or another, and
more and more men were asking themselves 'Why am I bothering?' as we rapidly
became no-hopers. The Japs were on the ground and the Allies in the air and on
the sea; how could we hope to beat such protagonists?

From Liang we moved to the town of Ambon on the southern leg of the island
and there we stayed overnight in a churchlike building; a most useful spot for our
prayer meetings. Of course, we could not expect even one night without fear or
excitement, and we now found ourselves in mortal fear of our first earthquake.
Subjected to heavy tremors inside and outside my body I said:

'I'm bloody fed up and wish I'd never joined, all we need now is a bloody
earthquake!'

Next day we continued across the bay and arrived at Wyjami camp amid strong
rumours that we were about to be shipped with others. Movement was a word I
understood only too well — since 1940 in France I had done little else other than
be 'up front'. This next move would be my most horrendous but I hoped that no
matter how difficult, it would not be my last; life was being pretty mean to us but
we still hung on to it. Having spent some five or six weeks on Ambon it would now
be about 14th September 1944, and still I looked for Ted, without success.

On 14th or 15th September we left camp by lorries to another camp which I
believe was Romah Tiga, and there we joined others waiting to embark. It was
there that I first heard about my other friend, Ron Taylor, who had left on a ship
from Liang with Flying Officer Heath, some time last May. The news I heard was
so revolting and hurtful that I fervently hoped it was but a rumour. How else could
such information reach us from Java except by the regular shipping runs of the
Japs themselves? However, as painful as it was I would have to accept it as truth at
a later date. We were at this camp for two or three days during which time I again

asked around for Ted, again without success. On the 17th we moved out to a ship in the harbour and I shall never forget my first sighting of that small ship we were about to board. By comparison. the infamous *Amagi Maru* had been a pleasure boat and my heart sank further.

The journey is best described by reference to the report our leader, Flight Lieutenant Blackwood, made to the War Crimes tribunal after the war. On the morning of our departure it had rained for the first time in many days. From the point where we had left our road transport, we marched, mostly barefoot and tattered, in a glutinous sea of liquid mud, which hid the sharp coral rock surface of the road. Guards hustled and harassed us along, and those crippled from beriberi were being pushed and bullied. The stretcher-bearers, themselves unfit, were being goaded into a shambling trot until eventually we reached a jetty. There, the stretchers were laid out on the mud, fully exposed to the pitiless rains. There were some empty huts nearby in which we were not allowed to shelter. After everyone had been soaked they produced a few straw mats, which we laid over those who were most ill. Their moans and groans fell without response upon the deaf ears of our guards.

After a wait of nearly three hours, barges were brought alongside. We were ferried out across the creek to where our sea transport lay at anchor. It was the infamous *Maros Maru*, a small diesel ship of wooden construction about 600 tons in weight. Apparently it had belonged to the Dutch, was scuttled in Tandjoeng Priok harbour and raised by the Japs in 1943. When we came alongside I thought this could not possibly be for our use as there was no way it could house or even hold five hundred men. Even worse was to follow as we saw that the holds were already battened down: we were to travel on deck, where even the sick people would be exposed to the fierce sun and tropical storms, without any cover whatsoever. Any possessions had to be placed on the hatch covers. An attempt was made to distribute a number of semi-fit men amongst the sick, in gangways and in narrow deck spaces. Very sick men were subjected to extreme discomfort and it was already clear that many would not sustain this journey. Trying to find a decent space was almost impossible yet there was worse to come — firewood for the journey was brought alongside to share our space. Imagine a small ferry boat with a maximum beam (breadth) of not more than thirty feet. The length available for the complete party was no more than forty feet; the deck housings and workings were out of bounds. From that can be judged the measure of overcrowding.

The Japs used the forward cabins in the forecastle (crews quarters), and there was a machine gun mounted on the deck above them. Every movement by prisoners, crew or guards was made by 'tip-toeing' between bodies and firewood on the main deck. We had to remove firewood from a space in front of the small bridge section. This revealed a door through which the guards would come, whenever required to encroach upon our space. There was another large door on one side of the ship which I imagine was used for entry and loading, or, as the Japs demonstrated, for a sudden exit. We were left with no option but to rest ourselves on the bundles of firewood stacked around the ship's sides and up to the gunwales (top of the ship's sides). Two familiar wooden boxes were slung over the sides, intended for latrine uses. Each time we headed for those boxes it was fraught with difficulty trying to find a way between all the obstacles. It was much worse for those who were bad on their legs, who kept falling and tripping at every step.

As the anchor was raised a Liberator bomber was seen heading towards the harbour and docks. Suddenly it changed its course toward our small ship and almost lazily it headed in a direct path to sit right above us.

'Oh Good God, this is how it ends,' I thought, 'Are we never to be left alone in peace?'

It hadn't bombed the docks so we had to be its target. That seemed a fair assessment so we primed ourselves and prayed once more. Praying seemed to have become a daily occurrence and this particular prayer was answered when the aircraft turned away and disappeared into the distance. We thought maybe it had no bombs so had decided to reconnoitre and take pictures. We were left wondering whether the navigator or pilot had seen the many bodies on the deck and assuming them to be Pow's or natives, had left us alone. Or would the next day see him return to take care of us when we reached the open seas, to leave no survivors to tell our tale? It seemed we had little time left for optimism. However, those worries were soon alleviated when we heard the sound of dropping bombs and saw a great plume of smoke, maybe oil tanks. The pilot had found a suitable target.

It was evening when we left the harbour. It was rumoured that we were sailing for the island of Baru which lay directly to our west, a short distance across the Banda sea. That first night at sea was a real nightmare. At first choppy, it then became rough, gathering force until it reached a state of tempest. Water swept across the deck with each and every roll of the ship, and even the matloes amongst us suffered badly. Helpless bodies were tossed on top of each other and stretcher cases were thrown about like flotsam as everything and everyone seemed to be colliding. The storms sent our 'brave' guards to their life jackets, and they huddled together close to their exit door ready to abandon ship, and us. We had reached the time for deep thought.

If I forget

O' Lord thou knowest
How distraught I am
If I have forgotten thee
I pray that you do not
Forget me
In this time of
My desperate need.

Anon.

The first prisoner died that night on the *Maros Maru.*

When we had embarked we were already worn out by fifteen months of slavery, starvation, cruelty and the resulting malnutrition. Our plight was worsened on board with constant ill-treatment, fear of the unknown, and never knowing which moment was to be your last. Then beriberi became our number one scourge. Day after day men who were grievously ill were laid on the hatch covers, exposed to the pitiless tropical sun followed by the cold of night. Our Leader, Flight Lieutenant Blackwood, had made regular complaints and requests for some sort of awning to shade the very ill. It was not until thirty men had died that he met with any success. For all they cared they might not even have been aware of our presence on that bloody ship. After the thirty deaths from dehydration and exposure, the makeshift awning was erected. It would still only cover the very worst of the sick on the hatch covers.

After the second night it appeared that our destination of Baru island had been more 'duff gen'. No doubt we sailed *close* to Baru but we did not stop there. We sailed directly west heading in the general direction of the Celebes, always staying very close to land. After the initial thirty, the deaths continued at a rate of one or two a day. Then we had a mishap at one of the latrine boxes; a lad had visited a box where it was necessary to negotiate over and around a ship's rail. The lad was unsuccessful and fell overboard. At once the shouts of 'man overboard' echoed around the ship. We had never been more surprised than when the ship turned about and was able to pick the lad up. It was the first voluntary act of decency we had ever witnessed, and I'm afraid we tended to believe the Indonesian helmsman had acted upon his own volition.

The Japs pushed the man straight back to us, firmly chastised but without the usual slappings. Naturally, they did not wish to be denied some punishment nor did they wish to be seen going soft, so they took their retribution on the officers who were called to the small bridge area, and made to kneel whilst a guard went along beating them with a ship's rope. On bare and sore backs of men already weak, it was not enjoyed except by our sadistic enemy. The reason for the punishment was for not being in control of the poor devil who had fallen overboard. At this time, many of the guards were still being sea-sick — they made a sorrowful example of fit men.

An undercurrent of whispering had started amongst the prisoners:

'Could we take over the ship?'

We seemed to be in a favourable location geographically and would never be closer to freedom ever again: to the north lay the Philippines, and a shorter distance to the east was New Guinea, with many smaller islands dotted about. The problem was that we had no idea where the Allies were. However, an Allied submarine or aircraft might spot us if we displayed a suitable signal but so may the Japs and that would mean 'lights out' for certain. It seemed that because we had so little to lose, these often insane ideas were fostered and they raised a little hope. This present gamble would have depended on the position of New Guinea which would be the better place to head for. I believe the plan was finally passed to our senior officer, because understandably many were against the plan. One or two had actually threatened to 'talk' if any move went ahead. In the final analysis it was decided against, on the grounds that the Allies were unlikely to have progressed so far, and the idea was dropped. However, the talk and thoughts had done a little good to our ego and resistance — for a little while it had made 'lions' out of we 'sheep'.

On 21st September 1944, we arrived at Raha Moena in the Celebes. We had not been there many hours when we met another party of 128 Allied prisoners who had left Ambon two or three days before ourselves and had now come from a place named Kendari on the east coast of the Celebes. The party had already lost twelve men when they went through a very frightening and traumatic experience. They had left Ambon Town in a small wooden boat named *Haruyshi Maru* which was extremely overcrowded; many were suffering from dysentery and had to be kept in a corner of the deck in an attempt at isolation. With no medical people or any services, the sick had lain in wretched conditions and in their own filth. At one point early into the journey their boat started to leak, and the water rose in the bilges stopping the engines. Together they managed to contain the water at a safe level until reaching Kendari where they stayed a day and a night.

They were transferred to another boat at midday; that same day they were strafed by a four-engined bomber about a mile from the shore. Apparently an American bomber had come into sight and, as with a predecessor, had circled taking a look around. It seemed that the crew were trying their best to determine whether or not the ship was hostile and worth sinking. On the other hand, knowing prisoners were being moved from place to place, they would possibly have left it alone once men were seen on board. After a careful look and without interference from the ship, the aircraft made as though to leave the scene — until one stupid bloody Jap put his oar in. This headstrong guard either panicked or simply wanted to draw first blood, and he fired at the aircraft with tracer bullets. Without further ado the pilot turned his aircraft and attacked with cannons and guns blazing from every quarter.

The small boat was virtually cut into two halves, everyone had to abandon ship and the prisoners were left to their own devices. The semi-fit men must have done a really man-sized job, turning their unselfish thoughts to the sick, for they lost only eight men, killed by gun fire. LAC Hugh Black picked up, amongst others, a Corporal Mann who was dead, though without any outward sign of injury. It was as though he had died of drowning or of aggravated shock. Another man helped by Hugh Black was an airman named Jefferies who had a bad leg wound — unfortunately he died on the beach. Flying Officer Mason, and Airmen Lawton and Topliss stayed on the ship until all the sick prisoners had been helped into the water. All those who made shore were collected up by the Japs later and handed over at Raha. Their losses *en route* were Corporals Ramsden and Warwick and LAC Preece, all RAF — they were buried alongside Squadron Leader Hopkins, A/B Hooper, McGann (RASC) and a Dutchman, at Raha. Two other Dutchmen plus Corporals Pepper, Higgins and Lennon, all RAF, were missing presumed drowned.

On 22nd September 1944, the *Maros Maru* left Raha Moena for Macasser. A day or two later men began to die even more quickly, as conditions had deteriorated even further with the addition of the extra passengers but no extra rice. The water issue was reduced to less than half a pint a day whilst the Korean guards bathed in drums of drinking water. The seriously ill now completely cluttered the covered hatches; the open deck without any protection from tropical sun, and often heavy rains, held all the others, who were worsening due to thirst and exposure as well as beriberi. I had again started to ask myself how much time I had left — wishing no doubt that I could see my family and home just once more before beriberi dealt me its death-blow. Apart from the fact that we were all friends in deep trouble in this bizarre situation, except for Joe Connor I felt so awfully alone; and perhaps I did not fully understand the position I found myself in. I seemed fated to lose all my closest friends so it was now extremely important that Joe remained alive.

Crawling along the coastline of the Gulf of Boni, staying close to the shore, we continued our journey to Macassar hoping to remain unsighted by Allied aircraft. We prayed that the journey would speed up whilst we were still able to live and complete it. After one or two days' sailing, the ship's engines broke down in mid-ocean — leaving us a sitting duck for our 'friends' to pick off. The ship was crewed by Indonesians and Japs who between them had absolutely no technical knowledge of engines — it seemed the Devil himself sat on our shoulders. 'Here we go again', we must have thought. On board we had our dear friends Blood and Slime and the Haruku commandant Lieutenant Kurishima — as yet there had been no opportunity to heave them overboard; such a beautiful thought! Those three knew of the naval ratings who had been in their camp and were now on board the *Maros Maru*. Now that Jap lives were also at risk they had no qualms about asking for help from their 'useless slaves' — they had less principal and little honour when it came to the test.

When their first pleasant and oh so friendly 'request' came our way, no one answered their call for help.

'Let the Bastards sweat' and 'Wait until they come crawling' would best describe the unhelpful attitude, especially of the HMS *Electra* and HMS *Jupiter* lads. A sensible discussion reminded us all that we, too, were at even greater risk and responsible for many dying men who had little time left without help. The OK was eventually given to Petty Officer Platt and a couple of technical ratings to see what they could do. The petty officer placed his treasured peaked naval hat at the correct angle, drew himself up to his full height and called to the nearest Jap:

'Lead the way, mate.'

He was going to show them the Royal Navy were No 1, not the Japs nor their blessed 'Son of Heaven'.

We had two Palestinians (RAF) on board who, like ourselves, were prisoners living only on the revolting rice pap. One of them was laying over the ship's rails with his food tin in one hand and his spoon in the other, taking a spoonful of the glue-like mixture into his mouth, only for it to come back again and into the sea. He tried and tried, again and again, until finally he held it down. Never did he intend to stop trying and I thought to myself, what a fine and determined young man he was. He certainly was earning the right to survive and recapture his freedom — which, indeed, he did.

Scenes of indescribable horror continued until they became commonplace: men picked their way through the tangled mass of humanity which lay around the narrow ship; and orderlies carried the naked and wasted bodies of the dead to the side of the ship where men like Bill Lockwood (242 Squadron) and Bud Fisher of the 'waxed moustache', helped to cast the weighted bodies into the sea. Tongues began to blacken, and raw shoulders peeled and bled whilst the last drops of sanity left many men as each night was filled with the tortured yells and moans of the dying. They were joined by the curses of the more able who tried so hard to gain a little rest, hoping to sleep away their worries if only for an hour.

Some of the more chronically ill developed an awful sounding symptom that seemed to affect a man about to die of beriberi — a loud lasting period of violent hiccuping. Another youngster, delirious and distraught with sunstroke, shouted out the thoughts of a demented and distorted mind for thirty long hours before he became too weak to utter a single word. By this time men were dying like flies in the winter, their bodies being thrown overboard at regular intervals at the rate of about eight men each day. Most were helped on their way by that character Bud Fisher of the 3rd Hussars, whom I first noticed on Ambon, and whose reputation was as a 'wild man with a heart of gold'. He was continually teased about his moustache — a really grand specimen. Some will remember Bud and his friend whom he nicknamed 'Copperplate'. I hope that Copperplate will recognise himself in this story.

A cry went out: 'Hey, look at this' as a huge whirlpool-like movement appeared out at sea not too far from the starboard side of the ship. Apparently it was a most impressive sight to behold, but I found it impossible to reach starboard being unable to lift my legs over the many obstacles. A Japanese crewman tried to explain the phenomena. The vortex was huge, fascinating and gave off a fear-inspiring aura that all who watched would be sucked into its very centre and become lost forever. I dearly wished I could have seen the spectacle for such an opportunity would never come my way again.

Before the vortex, Copperplate had been leaning against those starboard rails lost to the world. He was feeling a total loneliness, a hopelessness during which he experienced a strong desire to let go and be done with the whole affair. It was a strange emotion which he found difficult to explain, but let him try:

'Leaning against the rails with not enough to eat or anything to drink, with men dying all around me and others being thrown overboard as though coming off a production line. Nothing to see except the ocean that tempts me into its whipped-up waves with its far horizon empty. Nowhere to go except this tiny space in the enemy's house and almost totally inactive. Nothing to talk about that hasn't been said many times before; almost a complete mental blackness with a strange desire to weep, to scream, then fall asleep never to waken again. A desire to plead with those beyond my reach to desist and for pity's sake leave me alone. A quiet feeling of 'to hell with it all' rather like the drunken man who is thoroughly saturated with drink and no longer has any desire except to close his eyes and sleep forever. A wish to separate oneself from the reality of the moment, maybe the wish is the one that precedes death on the passing of all mortals. Never before or since have I experienced such extremes of emotion, nor will I, and I still wonder if my friends passed through this same experience before they died — I believe they all did.'

On 6th October 1944, we arrived at Macassar, having travelled close to land by day and anchored at night, afraid to venture out onto the high seas. Whilst we were in harbour, which is best described as a number of very small islands clustered together, we were frequently attacked by Allied aircraft. Outside the harbour there was a constant submarine patrol cutting the Jap lines of communication and putting the Fear of God into us. Although coconuts and mangoes were brought aboard during this stopover, prisoners continued to die at an alarming rate. During that stay in Macassar harbour alone, 150 men died, twenty-two more than we had picked up at Raha Moena.

The dockside was in a very battered and rough state of repair. Having been a naval base it had seen much action during The Battle of the Java Seas. A burnt-out sugar storage shed was the first big find in the looting game of search and steal — the men were attracted to that sugar like bees to honey. Large lumps were furtively eaten and quietly lifted to save it falling into the hands of other would-be thieves. So much was eaten on the spot that it did no one any good at all; apparently, too much eaten in our condition was more harmful than helpful as pained stomachs later proved. But I suppose the immediate gratification justified such action, for that day was the only one we cared about.

A sigh of relief went up when, after replenishing their stores, the ship's anchor was raised. It is something of an enigma to say we wanted to get to sea and reach the comparative safety of Java as soon as possible, because at the same time we had no wish for the ship ever to leave land. However, the *Maros Maru* set sail and, having emptied her holds of many drums of petrol and mixed cargo, we could now use the extra space available for the sick who had to go down into another 'black hole'. Joe Connor and myself needed help to go below. At least during daylight hours it was a happy release from the strength-sapping and burning heat of a fearsome sun.

After a very short time the ship stopped and dropped anchor at a small island which may have been Pare-Pare in the Straits of Macassar. For some reason, we stayed marooned there for many days — horrendous days when ten and often twenty men a day were wrapped in anything that willing hands could find and then buried at sea. They were given the only honourable and Christian burial that was available — a few spoken words.

Few words were passing between Joe and I, most likely we were just praying to stay together; we were each other's crutch. Eventually, coverings for bodies ran out, and they were simply tied to any sort of weight that could be found before being placed in the water. By the second week disobedient bodies began to rise to the surface from their watery grave. It was macabre to see what may well have been a good friend saying:

'Why me? Please don't leave me here.'

The island was one of horror and dread as we all waited and wondered when it was to be our own turn, or thought that maybe this unreal nightmare would go away and we would find ourselves wakening from a long and disturbed sleep to find ourselves still at home and safe.

One night before we left this gruesome place, a young man, no more than twenty-one, started a spate of hiccuping — very loudly and at regular intervals. It really was not a pleasant noise. Mori made an appearance at long last, and he at once started his usual threatening attitude. He said he would beat the sick (that would have been a wholesale attack) unless the noise stopped and he didn't care how. With no alternative an orderly injected the man to shut him up. The injection lasted about half an hour and then the lad started again. He was given a further injection. For a third time the very sick man began yet again — he was dying and the cause was beriberi. Mori returned, further threatening anyone and everyone by promising to set upon the stretcher cases with his infamous bamboo, which he was quite capable of doing in his present mood. A third injection was given after which nothing more was heard from the lad — he had died from beriberi, as expected.

Our dash across the Java Sea saw us approaching Sourabaya on 23rd November 1944. We were about to enter the harbour when the last of Bud Fisher's clients found his watery grave. He was known to us as 'Tich', a Mancunian who had been ill for almost the whole journey. We were still capable of feeling sorrow for those who had desperately hung on so long, only to lose out in sight of a winning post, but it would happen to many others yet.

Joe and I had been in the ship's hold since leaving Macassar and were plagued by body lice — how they loved the warmth of our bodies! We continually attempted to rid ourselves of them only for them to hatch out more within the hour. Vermin were as equally difficult to bear as all the other hardships we endured.

I tried to help Joe with a little bullying because his spirits were so low — he was suffering so much pain from his complaint.

'Jim, I can't take much more of this, I've just about had it.'

That statement, or words of similar meaning, had been spoken many times before when life was ebbing from a weakened body. I felt the same but replied, probably automatically:

'Don't be so bloody daft, Joe, you haven't come all this way to let a few sodding Japs or pains beat you now.' And I continued: 'It's the bloody lice that have got you down and we'll soon be free of those, so pull yourself together.'

Joe, my other half, smiled and said:

'I suppose you're right but it would be easier to let go — I'll be OK now.'

I thought 'OK you may be, but I'm not': I couldn't feel my legs, even when I pinched them hard — they were both as dead as dodo's. We had now docked at the end of this 'unbelievable journey' which had lasted 68 days (in peacetime it would have taken 5 or 6 days). We had been living as scum in Japanese-created filth and disease. We had thought Haruku, with its 25 per cent death rate, was bad enough but on this journey we had made the 50 per cent mark. *Every other man died:* clinically murdered by inhuman indifference.

Those who survived were mere ghosts of their former selves and many were half-demented wrecks of humanity, diseased, filthy and crawling with vermin. On the given signal to offload I tried bracing myself ready to climb out of the hold and onto terra firma, knowing that something most unpleasant was happening to me. I was rather apprehensive. Could I get out of the hold? Would someone offer to help Joe haul me out? — I could not afford to be left in the hold. Perhaps I had become a little panicky. I tried standing on my feet only to go crashing down in a big heap on the floor; no one needed to tell me that I was paralysed from my waist down, a symptom of beriberi.

'For Christ's sake, Jim, what's the matter? We've got to get off this bloody ship,' said a concerned Joe, now forgetting his own troubles.

'I've had it Joe, you get out before you land in trouble.'

I was concerned that he would be further punished for aiding and abetting me. I had been careless enough to become useless like those Jap animals in their fields — my future may be very short. Another semi-fit lad came across as they usually did, and together they dragged and pushed me out. It hurt like hell and each movement was agony, but I was to be forever grateful to my pal(s).

I was placed amongst the sick on the dockside; I now qualified to be termed sick for I could no longer walk — that was the only Jap criterion for sickness. The others were then judged to be fit and ready for more of the same treatment. I was paralysed, hungry and dirty, and could not have felt more depressed than at that moment. I was now content to let fate have its way with me and I no longer wished to continue the battle — I was almost relieved by the thought. I was not to know that somewhere in most men, there is that something that drives us on in spite of odds; some call it guts. Right then I felt I had none. I had lost Joe No 2 now because he was a walker with the others, and that did not help my morale. Once more, I felt alone. The lads who had struggled through eighteen months of dreadful hell, then completed this awful journey, could easily be put on the next ship north, if I knew our captors. Those same lads would surely die of disease and starvation, or maybe drown. I feared I had seen the last of Joe Connor and Ted Chester — I was shattered.

The stretcher cases were pointed out by Kasiyama to be put, or rather slung, onto lorries while the others turned and ambled away as best they could. Some finished up in the Macasura camp and others in the infamous Cycle camp, both in Batavia. The journey from Sourabaya to Batavia had taken almost twenty-four hours, packed like cattle in a train. The sick 'useless animals' were now wondering if, after all the troubles of surviving, they were now to be written off; anything was possible. How was I to know that my prayers would be answered, at least in the short term?

I was heading for my 'Heaven on Earth'. Taken into the grounds of a large building and dumped on the grass, I was stripped of my only possession, my dirty old shorts, and in the 'nuddy' was hosed down with a strong disinfectant along with the other sick men. All old shirts and shorts were burned before we were placed on clean stretchers by other prisoners who were clean and almost properly dressed. I really couldn't understand. After nearly three years of captivity such as we had been subjected to, how could prisoners appear this way? It was only when I was finally carried into the building and put into a real bed that I realised I was in a hospital. I could not understand why prisoners were allowed into the only hospital I had ever seen or heard of. I believe I must have wondered if the war had ended whilst we were on that vile ship. If I did, then I expected far too much. More likely I was worried about being used for spare parts in some diabolical experiment, as it was often said and believed that our captors carried out dastardly and horrific experiments on prisoners — which was later proven.

Thirty-seven years later, a certain Naoji Uezono was to recall the pain of conscience felt over the medical experiments on humans which were conducted by his regiment, the 731st Unit. Many of those responsible swallowed poison pills rather than surrender and perhaps divulge the secret findings of their experiments. Others live to this day whose secrets were traded for their lives by the Allies. This took place at a vast complex south of Harbin, Manchuria, where 3,500 soldiers and civilians spent the war developing germ warfare skills unmatched by any other nation. Their expertise, which could have changed the course of the war if Hiroshima and Nagasaki had not happened, was acquired by experimenting on human guinea pigs — 'marula's' or 'logs of wood' as they were known to insiders.

There has never been the need to justify the use of those first two atomic bombs — nothing less would have penetrated their fanaticism. Dropping those bombs was no worse than the vivisection of thousands of Chinese, Russian and American prisoners, or the murder of thousands of Allied prisoners. Plus the fact they saved thousands more lives that would otherwise have been sacrificed during the inevitable invasion of the Japanese mainlands.

I soon realised that I was in St Vincentous Hospital, Batavia, which was the next best thing to being in Heaven — indeed I was very, very lucky. Now I could enjoy dying in a bed and the future could take care of itself so long as I remained there — hopefully for ever.

9. Heaven and Fear

If I was dreaming then I was convinced it would end; that I would awaken to find myself staring into the leering face of Bamboo Mori. Thank goodness it was not to be, for the face looking down on me was one I would never wish to forget: that of my earthly Patron Saint Tubby Parker, a medical orderly. To this day I remember him with gratitude, and his dedication towards others and myself in particular, should not go unsung.

The very first words I heard from Tubby were:

'Now then young man, we'll soon have you put right.'

Those words were not welcomed with the enthusiasm he had the right to expect.

'You needn't bloody bother,' was the nearest I can recollect saying, with a little more venom than was polite. I continued:

'There's no way I wish to leave this bed, ever.'

That was my final word, said with the deepest conviction. Very warmly and with great understanding Tubby said:

'I've seen many distressing cases come through this hospital though never worse than those coming in from Haruku and Ambon.'

I lay there now fully conscious of my surroundings, taking in all the luxury and the sweet smell of hospitalisation that just had to be my Heaven on Earth, and I was pleased I hadn't died on the *Maros Maru*. Still I implored Tubby to:

'Leave me alone please, I'm content just to be here.'

I remained apprehensive as the patient Tubby replied:

'Don't you realise that you are paralysed?'

'Of course I do, it's the only way I can cope and avoid another sea-going draft which would surely kill me.'

Still speaking my thoughts I continued:

'I'm quite happy to die in this bed and be clean when I go, so please leave me.'

Hell, I had only been off that bloody ship a few hours and here was someone only interested in getting me on another, or so it seemed to me; well he could go to hell! I was saying what I truly felt because I did not wish to continue my battle unless it became more equal. I felt no shame. I had already fought harder than many.

'OK, Jim, I'll do what I can to keep you here until you are on your feet and feel you can cope.'

That fellow was still being much more tolerant than I had the right to expect or ask, and I will never forget what I believe was his next comment:

'One thing worth remembering, Jim, is that the secret of living is to endure and so far you have proved that.'

I thought to myself 'what the hell does he know about endurance? Anyone who has not been on the islands, or on Jap transport at sea, can know anything about enduring.' The days passed and turned to months. Many times I thought of his words. I had endured all along and hadn't I said the very same things to my pal Joe? So was I being two-faced or hypocritical? If I gave up now it would have all been a wasted effort. Furthermore I would be letting down those who had battled on until they no longer had breath, when death overtook them. Tubby had got through to me at last and he was as good as his word, spending more time with me than I was entitled to.

St Vincentous. to the best of my knowledge. was the only hospital in the Indies where the Japs allowed prisoners to be treated. Perhaps it was their showpiece for any 'interfering' outsiders or Red Cross personnel. I had indeed been very lucky to finish up here; it was my lifesaver. Prisoners had to be in very bad shape before being allowed treatment. One's stay would only be as long as the Jap doctor was satisfied you could not stand unaided — the only measuring stick he would use.

Each day Tubby would come along with his usual good cheer and my painful punishment. I was still a little mixed up when he first began to massage my legs. It was really excruciatingly painful and an experience I would not wish to repeat, but he assured me it was part of very necessary treatment. I well remember blowing my top more than once saying things like:

'Listen Tubby, I couldn't care less about getting out, for God's sake leave my legs alone.'

Eventually, I suppose he thought it was time to be more firm with me so he laid down his law.

'Look Jim, whether you like it or not I have a job to do and I aim to do just that — so shut it.'

He certainly did that job and earned my eternal gratitude. I had been fortunate once again in that he had chosen to give me a little special kindness. Tubby asked me to co-operate and show just the amount of improvement he instructed daily — to keep the Jap doctor at bay — and I was a good pupil now having seen the light. After the first few days he would bring along a number of tablets and slip them discreetly into my hand saying:

'Keep these to yourself Jim and take them whenever you get the opportunity'. He continued:

'They are not official issue by the Japs and they know nothing about us having them so please be careful.'

I certainly did not need a second warning on that score.

I continued to forget all about the outside world, not caring too much for what it had to offer. I found it strangely easy to forget as I enjoyed my new-found comforts and I wasn't going to do anything except keep a low profile. Each day I received my tortuous treatment before the Jap doctor did his rounds and I quickly noticed how early he sent men out into the prison camps once they showed signs of recovery. Each afternoon a camp lorry would arrive and ferry them back into the real world of Jap camps. There would sometimes be words between our doctors and the Japs; often quite fierce opposition was presented by our doctor, as he attempted to protect his patient. However, only limited argument could take place before the Jap doctor sensed he was about to 'lose face'; his face would colour up which was a very good warning to terminate any argument. Other signs would always follow: one or two snarls and a rising blood pressure were all signals to cool it. To do otherwise would doubtless lead to a few additional discharges of more unfit men and, perhaps, a slapping for good measure. Our doctors and their staff seemed to have everything under control within a sound and sensible policy; it was not for patients such as myself to foul things up for others.

There existed a useful 'Jungle Telegraph' between the hospital and the outside camps, so I asked Tubby to try and find out if my friends Ted Chester and Tom Elgey, or any 242 Squadron lads, were in those camps. If they were and I was lucky enough, I may yet catch up with some of them. At the same time I selfishly hoped it would not happen for some time yet whilst I was so comfortable. Right then I wouldn't have called the King my uncle!

Tubby and I talked about the time spent on Haruku, Ambon and about the journeys on two hell ships. He knew something of it from those who had been through his hands earlier.

'Jim,' he said, 'I never would have believed that any human could treat another with so much indifference. It would have been kinder to have shot you all than stand purposely by, watching men wither away.'

He spoke such words with the true feelings of one who cared and understood each word. He continued:

'One party came back from Haruku, some of whom were blind, whilst others had every conceivable tropical disease you could mention — most had forms of malnutrition.' I knew which party he was speaking of. It had left us on 25th November 1943 with Martin, Pat and Paddy McQuade in it: Pat McGrogan had certainly been in a bad way and Martin Oldfield was almost blind.

My progress continued very slowly resulting from my mature acting ability. Weeks passed and as yet *Dai Nippon* had not pointed his finger at me, and mine remained firmly crossed. Tubby usually accompanied the doctors when they did their rounds and when they reached me Tubby would gaze at me with a look of despair as though to say I was a lost cause. At the same time, following his instructions, I would look non-plussed and parhaps a little *non compos mentis*; I had been well trained by Tubby who understood the strange mentality of the Jap medics. I didn't understand any of them; I simply despised them all for taking the lives of so many friends. Our doctors understood that, unless more urgent cases required a bed, it was essential to give the likes of myself as much time as they were able, before we had to start out yet again on some diabolical slave party.

The day came which was really mine; the 'Jungle Telegraph' had answered and I received good news. Both Ted and Tom were said to be in Cycle camp. I was overjoyed that one of our combine and my oldest friend were both still alive. I always knew Tom had an old head on his shoulders and, true to form, he had not even been out of Batavia. The news told me that Ted was not well but I knew him better than most and realised that at any time he looked weak, when in fact he was wiry and tough as teak. To any outsider he may have looked half dead but his image gave lie to that inner strength, so I wasn't despondent.

My Swindon-born and earthly 'Saint Tubby' cared for me throughout the weeks and months that followed whilst I regained much of my original fitness and, more importantly, the will to go on. We had to part the day he could no longer cover for me without exposing others to some risk. That day *Dai Nippon* stood by my bed looking me up and down; my fate depended upon his next few words. The dreaded answer came:

'Him OK, go campo.'

Perhaps I should have those words printed on my headstone for they said it all. I was discharged to face whatever remained of my immediate future. I could not disguise the feeling of having aged ten years in a single moment. Every sea-going cruise imaginable had my name on it as it sailed past my eyes and finished up in Davy Jones' locker, whilst bound for Singapore, Sumatra or even the ignoble land of the rising sun itself, perish the thought. I was a little frightened to face that same music once more.

After four months I now felt as fit as I could expect to be. Unfortunately it made me a number one candidate for the next draft out of Java. As far as I knew, I had no one in the camp that could bring any influence to bear on my behalf. Anyway, most of those in the camp would be established there and, in various ways, looking after number one. I must have shivered and quaked at the thought of being drowned after all that had passed, for the seas around Java were now known to be a minefield, with Allied submarines in complete control. Could I be blamed for being a little apprehensive, if not scared stiff? I was told that Sumatra was attracting a lot of labour and having experienced that country with its dense jungle and swampland, to say nothing of its wild animals, it would be a real killer for some. News that the last draft out of Batavia had been sunk with all hands lost somewhere in the Sunda Straits, did nothing to ease the worries.

'So long Jim and take care', were the last words Tubby and I expected to share — but they were not, thank goodness. I know he understood how I felt towards him and the gratitude I would always have. It was the feeling of brotherhood that so many Fepow's shared, cemented forever. With some concern and trepidation, I climbed that camp lorry guarded by a familiar Korean whom I had tried so hard to forget. He took just one disdainful look at me before he launched into his expected hysterical gibberish,

'Kono Yaro. Piggi Lecas,' (Stupid fool. Move fast.)

One look at the almost permanently sneering face reminded me that things were now back to the norm.

I was taken to Cycle camp where, upon arrival, I was simply told to park my body somewhere and leave my service particulars. However, I was clean and wearing a new shirt and shorts so I shouldn't grumble. It was now April 1945 — already three years had passed since being taken prisoner — when I went looking for my lost friends in the camp. Ted, Tom, Pat and Martin should be in the camp, what a reunion! If only Bill Pollock and Ron Taylor could have been with us. The thoughts were fantastic, until I was further rocked back on my heels; we were never allowed to feel good for long. Apparently, a draft had recently left, rumoured for Sumatra — the only consolation was that I had missed it by some weeks. It was a real set-back to find that all my friends, except Ted Chester, had been unlucky enough to be on that draft. More than one unfortunate who returned from Haruku and Ambon would have asked himself why he was being sent out again while many fit-looking men in those camps had never moved. Bill Pollock had left Ambon on the *Suez Maru*, a ship that carried many wounded Japs and was said to have been sunk with all hands lost. But I still clung to the hope that Bill might one day turn up, though it was said that a small ship had machine-gunned prisoners in the water.

I walked up slowly behind Ted as he talked to one of his friends, another local named Reece Richards. I hadn't met Reece before, unless it was in Ambon. He was a nice fellow, quiet and somewhat reserved yet not introvert. Ted and I must have looked an odd couple as we hugged and embraced each other, each believing the other had been lost for ever. A very strong bond had developed between us which is common to many Fepow's, except the few loner's. It is difficult to describe that spirit of friendship which was never to die over the years that have followed. Certainly it needed the most unusual and difficult environs in which to give birth to and cement such friendships. Ted's health wasn't too bad; I think whoever had answered my 'Jungle Telegraph' call had found the wrong person. Ted and I were soon back into our old combine routine, looking to volunteer for any outside working party that may provide 'loot'; we were not going to lose that habit for some time!

The camp population was a very mixed bunch with many crafty and wide boys; the long term residents of Java who always managed to stay put and avoid drafts. Life doesn't change much, whatever the nationality. I refer of course to those who were fit, not the unfortunates who were unable to undertake certain tasks.

My life continued in Cycle camp until a few days before my birthday, the 24th May. Now an ageing twenty-four year old, my supposedly best years were lost forever. Rumours were circulating, and if anything created and encouraged gossip it was:

'There's a draft going out.'

Those regular avoiders would be busy scurrying around to ensure their 'minders' had their safety in hand. At that period the 'Harukeans' and the Ambon lads were most concerned, for as new boys in the camp we knew we were surplus to camp requirement.

The unfriendly sea once more beckoned us into its clutches. It would be true to say that most of us were very apprehensive, if not scared, at the prospect of a third encounter with the ocean which most knew or felt would be their last. The news came abruptly when we were told: 'You are on a draft about to leave.'

On the 21st we moved out and I fully expected to be on a cruise for my birthday. Mercifully we were put on a train not to the docks of Tandjoeng Priok, but to Bandoeng — try to imagine the sheer joy and ecstasy of that moment for it was, and still is, indescribable. At Bandoeng I learnt that many of those who had returned with me on the *Maros Maru* in November 1944 had been drafted again within a couple of months, as I had feared. Others were in the camp at Bandoeng. Whilst I had been in hospital, my friend, Joe Connor, and others had gone to Singapore and Sumatra. I was now close to the place where I had been captured just over three years previously — it seemed an age.

The Bandoeng camp was not large and consisted mainly of brick buildings without windows. In each building fifty to sixty prisoners were berthed on a tiered system. Already I could not understand why we had been sent there, as few outside working parties were required. We had our *Tenko* at about 6.30am.

This camp was about 2,000 feet above sea level and the mornings started quite cold. With Haruku being so near the equator and extremely hot during daylight hours, we were not yet fully acclimatized to the cold and we found if difficult. Bandoeng had been famed as the cultural centre of Java; the quinine industry used the bark of the cinchona tree which was grown there on large plantations. As we moved about in the occasional work party we saw what a delightful place it was, more so than Batavia.

Although the roads were wide and nicely laid out, there were still distinct signs of Jap neglect and plunder. Nothing appeared to have been put back into the industry or the quality of life for the indigenous people. On one occasion we saw what looked like a huge crater just outide the town that had steam hissing from it as though from a hot spring. I have since learnt that it was called the 'upside down boat' though I cannot recall it resembling anything like that.

Ted and I, still together, went out in a wood party taking bundles of wood from the station yard into a women's camp. Thankfully I only once went into the women's camp, for the squalor in which they were forced to exist, along with children of all ages, was totally inexcusable, though by now expected. In the short time before our capture and the very early days in captivity, we had developed a great respect for the Dutch ladies. Many of them had incurred the wrath of and many painful slappings from the Japs as they attempted to pass over a little food or a cigarette before they too were locked up. Clear attempts had been made in the women's camps to both humiliate them and offend their dignity, without much success. I can remember no other work in Bandoeng camp apart from clearing up some houses after the Japs had used them; unfortunately they left nothing useful behind.

The only other incident I had recorded from this camp happened, I'm certain, in the month of July just before we left. It was the beating up of our senior officers. One evening at *Tenko* the Japs had demanded a list of skilled men. Names from the British section were not forthcoming so Kasiyama ordered all officers to the Jap guardroom to be given the third degree. Then, up came His Highness Blood(y) Mori whom I hadn't seen since leaving the *Maros Maru*. The sea journey had not mellowed him in any visible way; and demanding to know what was going on he took over.

It looked to be yet another set-up job. Mori started screaming and bawling in his own inimitable way, then, surprisingly, he dismissed them all, only to call back the most senior officers within minutes of having been dismissed. Mori then proceeded to beat up about fifteen officers individually, and at one time there were three officers lying on the ground, unconscious. Mori then made a special attack on Wing Commander Maguire, the officer who had been so well thought of by us in Sumatra and Java before capitulation. He was hit by a chair which fortunately broke, for it was very heavy and may otherwise have badly injured him; as it was he was only knocked out. Whilst Mori was having his grand slam Kasiyama was following around 'mopping up' with his fists and feet any officer on the ground. We had christened those two well; the title of Blood and Slime could not have suited them better.

At *Tenko* in mid-August 1945 we noticed many of the guards were new faces, and over the next few days the old familiar faces were not seen at all. There had to be some significance in such moves, but what? There were always many schools of thought or worry. The optimists, now only few in number, suggested there had been a 'clear out' of our old guards to avoid recognition when the Allies invaded the island. The pessimists were equally certain they had gone on a few days' leave before taking us on our last journey, maybe into the mines of Japan or a watery grave. At these times it was good to be a so-called fatalist as I was, because to take what comes when you have no option is the easiest decision to make.

Another noticeable thing was that the guards had started to patrol outside the camp and not inside as previously. This move may have suggested yet another source of trouble which had began to worry us — that of insurgents. Ted and I could have done a roaring trade with a stock of anti-depressant tablets or tranquilizers! The strange thing was that the new guards did not seem so heavy-handed; it was as though they still wished to thump us, all six, seven or eight stone of us, but held back for no apparent reason.

We had seen one or two parades of Indonesians escorted by a Jap soldier at each end of their column. They looked to be units of Indonesian youth and they carried banners of a political nature with the word 'Merdeka' (freedom) very prominently displayed. A number of most unusual things were no doubt taking place. Unfortunately it led to many rumours, none of which restored our faith in human nature. Again, I find it impossible to describe the highly-charged tensions that existed amongst us at crucial times. We were in total ignorance of what was happening outside of Java. Many prisoners had simply put any thought of home right out of their head, being certain there could not possibly be a safe way out of our dilemma. There was talk of a 'big bomb' having been dropped somewhere, but no one was sure where, or even if it was the truth. At that time our understanding of a 'big bomb' would have been something like a thousand-pounder — so what was so special about this one? No one had ever split an atom nor was it possible — at least that was the considered opinion of our intelligentsia. They were reminded by others that in times of war the sciences and inventive minds make progress much quicker than in normal times — maybe it could be an atomic bomb.

The why's and wherefore's, pro's and con's, were very much in charge of our thoughts and beliefs as we so needed to believe in such a phenomenon. It seemed that only a 'miracle' like that could give us back our freedom. The frightening thought associated with the dropping of an atomic bomb was how long we would be allowed to live afterwards. We would also have given thought to those innocent and long-suffering women and children on the Japanese mainland who would have met with horrendous deaths or injury. However, the guilt for such a catastrophe can only be laid at the door of their own Military who sowed the seeds of this hostility at Pearl Harbour on their day of infamy. Yet how was it possible to be at all optimistic, when only days earlier Blood and Slime had beaten up our senior officers, one of whom was later found to have a broken jawbone? Maybe those two obnoxious creatures had not heard the news; their acts of recent days had certainly not suggested peaceful thoughts.

On about 17th August 1945 were were called to *Tenko* and the Jap commandant put in a rare appearance. He read from a script he had prepared which, when interpreted, finished up saying:

'The war is over, you will soon be back with your friends and families.'

I suppose one would expect that statement to have caused an uproar of noisy happiness; in fact it would have been more noisily received by a horde of zombies. There must have been many differing thoughts of disbelief and distrust passing through the prisoners' minds — afraid to believe anything or anyone. We found it impossible to believe that these particular captors could suddenly talk this way, so calmly and without rancour. It simply had to be some cruel move; maybe a way to get us out of camp more quietly for their dastardly purposes. We had accepted it as a fact that total elimination of prisoners before the end of the year would happen, because of our limited use and their inability to feed us without creditable end product. We were much too weary and distraught to become excited. We now felt that only seeing could ever be believing.

We returned to our huts to talk amongst ourselves in apprehensive whispers as though being listened to. We tried to convince each other of the possible truth. There were no signs of earlier sadism being repeated, nor were guards rushing around to grab the first *samurai* sword to commit *Hara-Kiri*, as would have been expected. It was rumoured a few days later that the first atomic bomb, named

'Little Boy', had been dropped on Hiroshima on the morning of 6th August. It was a rumour we heard some nine days after it had happened. It had apparently been seen as the 'light of a thousand suns' and resulted in the deaths of over 200,000 people.

About the second or third week into August we were marched from the Bandoeng camp to the local station for a return journey to the infamous Cycle camp. Unknown to us at that time, the camps in central Java were already at grave risk of attack by Indonesian insurgents. Indeed, in later action between these rebels and the invading British forces, prisoners in this area were killed by the insurgents whilst still in their prison camps. I guess that is what many of us would call 'fate', saying, 'There but for the grace of God go I.'

Back in Cycle camp the news was known to be authentic as they had a hidden radio in the camp — the Japs had accepted defeat on 14th August 1945. We were now prepared to accept that as fact, but we were just as far from freedom as ever. Our camp CO knew all that was happening and already had contact with the RAPWI (Returning Allied Prisoners of War and Internees) people in Singapore. He also knew only too well the reason for the howling mobs of Indonesians at our camp fences. We did not know whether to watch out more for the Japs or the Indonesians for our personal health and well being. Most frightening was the howling mob outside the camp for they would only see us as white and therefore Dutch, their enemy.

Mid-August was to be a most dreadful time, and goodness knows we had plenty of bad times to choose from, but now it was different — it was after the war had been won. We should now have been able to relax, regain composure and find our true selves once more, sit back and wait for our repatriation in peace and quiet, and perhaps say:

'Well done, mate, we've made it at last.'

But it was not yet to be. Instead we were now seriously threatened with death at the hands of a third party with whom we had no quarrel. Outside our barbed wire fences at all times their banners fluttered and fists threatened. Their freedom word, 'merdeka', mocked us as it poured from every mouth as if to say:

'This is our freedom, not yours.'

Only the presence of our recent brutal captor stood between us.

On the 15th the Jap commandant handed over his authority, though only on paper. The Japs were then instructed to maintain an armed presence and to give us protection from the insurgents. What a crazy mixed-up world we were living in. Days did not pass quickly enough and our sleep was restless. We now believed we would remain Jap prisoners until repatriated to Singapore, in the interests of our own safety.

The Javanese nationalism was now rampant and appeared to be beyond Japanese control. No doubt the Japs were most carefully fanning the flames. There was still time for our captor to implement his instructions for our elimination. Now that the Jap influence had been greatly neutralised there was nothing to fill the vacuum except, of course, the Javanese themselves. At last it was to be their day; the Dutch had been seen off and now the Japs were down — no one else would be allowed to fill that vacuum.

The people of the Indies had not received the freedom they had been promised, as the Japs, not surprisingly, had failed to provide a 'greater Asian prosperity'. Indeed, they had been more harshly treated by the Japs than by their previous

Dutch masters who had done a great deal for Java. The insurgents were now stirring their emotions to a fever pitch, and it was ironic that our brutal sadistic guards were now our only protectors. How far they would go in our defence remained to be seen, and worried about. Along with most others, I was very sceptical. How could they, overnight, change their attitude towards us from one of intense hatred to that of a friendly neighbour? With their obvious obsequious behaviour, they were clearly demonstrating an inherent hypocrisy.

It seemed that all those proverbial nine lives had now been used up and we were on borrowed time. Then, to our great delight, the first Red Cross parcels saw the light of day. A small number were taken from huge stocks which the Japs had deliberately kept from us, preferring to allow prisoners to die of starvation. Our own people rightly allowed only one parcel between four to avoid further damage to unhealthy, and now small, stomachs. Most parcels had already been opened by the Japs and certain items pilfered. The remainder had been left abandoned, to waste. The wonders of that food possibly meant more to us in those moments than the thoughts of an escape to freedom.

10.   Race to Stay Alive

In no way were we prepared to encourage the false friendship offered by our captors and our officers made them aware of this. Perhaps it was as well that our CO saw fit to post a standing order for all to see. It included the following:

'Anyone attempting to molest a Japanese soldier will be severely disciplined'!

On 8th September 1945, seven RAPWI officers parachuted into Java and were met by an unfriendly, if not actively hostile, reception. Then the facts began to emerge. The Japs, seeing that defeat was inevitable, hoped to create maximum difficulty for any Allied occupation force, so earlier on they had begun to encourage the Indonesian desire for independence. Consequently, a Republic of Indonesia was proclaimed by Doctor Soekarno on 17th August, a mere three days after the Japs had accepted defeat in Tokyo. Furthermore, tens of thousands of Japanese troops in Java and Sumatra handed over their weapons to the insurgents and quietly retired into a self-imposed internment. There were still no signs of a mass *Hara-Kiri*.

When representatives of the Dutch Government arrived at Batavia to take control on 15th September 1945, Dr Soekarno had already had a month in which to organise his Government forces: a *fait accompli* faced the Allied occupation forces. The intention of the Dutch Government was to resume control of the Dutch East Indies as they had left it in 1942. If there was any underlying intention to introduce liberal reforms, then no intimation of this was made known to the indigenous peoples prior to the arrival of SEAC (South East Asia Command) forces. In consequence, the attitude of the new Indonesian Government towards the Dutch was one of hostility, and towards the British forces, a deep suspicion. It was understandably thought that the role of the British was to hand back the East Indies to Dutch control as soon as RAPWI had completed its work and the Japanese forces were removed. Political confusion was now complete and it was under these highly dangerous conditions that the work of the occupation forces had to commence.

On 15th September 1945, HMS *Cumberland*, flying the flag of Rear Admiral W H Patterson, reached Batavia carrying the No 6 RAPWI control staff. No sooner had the cruiser docked at Tandjoeng Priok than the leader of the small team, which had earlier parachuted into Java, came aboard. He gave the Admiral a clear but intensely disturbing report of the military, economic and political situation. The country was clearly in chaos with little or no transportation and severe shortages, together with an extreme danger to the tens of thousands of prisoners. If signs of Dutch military action became apparent, these prisoners would be used as hostages, with a grave risk to their lives.

After the comparatively peaceful landing of a British Brigade the situation in Sourabaya deteriorated rapidly; this was largely due to increasing suspicion that

Canadians of 242 Squadron in France, May 1940.

Evacuating on the MS *Sobiesky* from St Nazaire to Folkestone, 1940.

Tom Elgey.

242 Group in Java before
capture, February 1942.

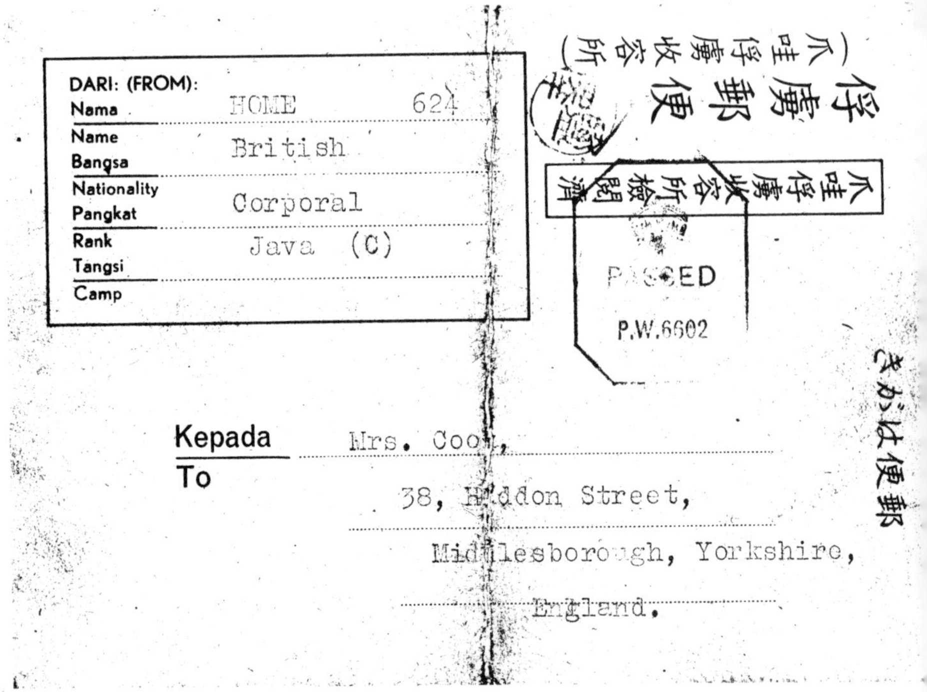

DARI: (FROM):		
Nama	HOME	624
Name		
Bangsa	British	
Nationality		
Pangkat	Corporal	
Rank	Java (C)	
Tangsi		
Camp		

侍　侍
虜　虜
收　收
容　容
所　所
檢
閲
濟

PASSED

P.W.6602

さ　か　は　便　郵

Kepada
To

Mrs. Coo

38, Haddon Street,

Middlesborough, Yorkshire,

England.

And the Japanese could not fill forms in either!

Mk I

Hurricanes of 242 Squadron being prepared for return
to England from France, June 1940

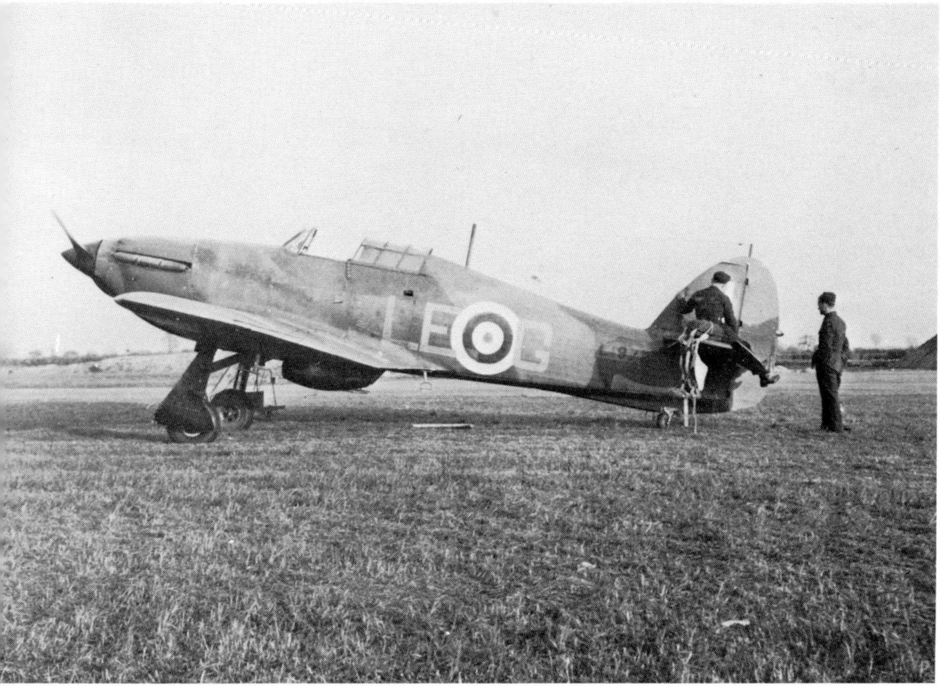

Mk IIA

The success of No 242 Fighter (Canadian) Squadron of the Royal Air Force has been well documented and is now historical fact. The squadron was the very first Command of that tenacious leader of men, Douglas Bader. There were other squadrons equally successful, but none more proud of their achievements than those of 242. We believed that it had the greatest set of men led by the most irrepressible leader. Enough has not been written or said of the mutual respect between such pilots of men led by the most irrepressible leader. Enough has not been written or said of the mutual respect between such pilots and the groundstaffs — a most important ingredient for success. 242 was as a family, close and protective of one another during the 'Battle of Britain'. The strong though not total 'Canadian' influence went some way towards the development of that feeling. Only a handful of its pilots survived the 'Battle' in the air and they were then posted out to the 'Far East' in 1941 where they had to fight their new 'battle' for survival, this time on the ground.

Twelve weeks on special food produces
much puppy fat.

The author with 242 Squadron's
emblem.

Cemetery on Ambon where the bones of the Haruku victims were re-interred.

Site of Boot Hill, Haruku, 1980.

Sir Douglas Bader, CBE, DSO, DFC.

On the way to the War Crimes Tribunal, September 1945, having not taken the honourable way out.

Ex-Harukeans released from River Valley Camp, Singapore.

Charges to pay

s. _____ d,

RECEIVED

POST OFFICE

No.

OFFICE STAMP

24 OCT

TELEGRAM

Prefix. Time handed in. Office of Origin and Service Instructions. Words.

14

m

m

414 C CW WPA 425 SINGAPORE 18 OCT

= COOK 38 HADDONSTREET MIDDLESBROUGH :

= AM SAFE IN BRITISH HANDS HOPE TO BE HOME
SOON WRITING REPLY CARE OF PO BOX 164
LONDON EC 1 = COOK

For free rep + 38 BOX 164 EC 1 + s ENQUIRY" or call, with this form B or C
at office of delivery. Other enquiries should be accompanied by this form, and, if possible, the envelope

the British were hand in glove with the Dutch. The difficulty the Indonesians found in distinguishing between the British and Dutch Military was a real problem. The deterioration was greatly exacerbated two days after the landing when Brigadier Mallarby, the Brigade Commander, was brutally murdered while engaged in negotiations with Indonesian leaders.

At the same time a small party of RAF officers, led by Wing Commander Kerr, had flown down from Batavia. They were ambushed and captured on the road from Sourabaya airfield to the town. The party were flung into jail in appalling conditions for two days, before being released. They were extremely lucky to escape with their lives. It was just another example of being confused with the Dutch forces, but Wing Commander Kerr eventually managed to convince his captors (Indonesians) that he was Australian and the rest of his party were British airmen.

The concentration of prisoners and internees in Sourabaya, Semerang and Batavia, and their subsequent evacuation from those parts, had been going well. But concern was felt for several thousands of unfortunates who were still incarcerated in various camps in Central Java. It was known that they were in a pitiable condition and were virtually held hostage eight months after the war had ended. Even if sufficient forces had been available to rescue them by military operations, it was almost certain that they would have been murdered by their captors before help could reach them. Withdrawal from the Dutch East Indies brought to an end the many difficult tasks that had faced SEAC forces in August 1945. It had taken fifteen months to rescue and repatriate the many thousands of APWI's from their terrible conditions; none were worse than those in the East Indies. All Japanese forces had been disarmed and, if not repatriated, were at least concentrated for eventual repatriation.

On 12th September 1945, a Flying Fortress flew over our camp at long last. It came in so low that we were concerned for its safety and after its second pass it dropped leaflets around the camp and over the airfield. We were advised that very soon a relief party would arrive; in the interim we were to obtain transport and go to the airfield at a given time the next day when they would drop us more supplies. The Japs obtained the transport and white material with which to mark out a dropping zone: no one needed to be asked to stick around and receive such wonderful goodies!

A small volunteer convoy set out after morning 'pap', protected by an armed force of Japanese soldiers. Our party was a volunteer one, for a number of men preferred to stay in what they considered the comparative safety of the camp. With the dropping zone suitably marked out, we waited with all the calm we could muster, like excited children let loose, but with the occasional glance over the shoulder. Eventually we heard the drone of the Fortress's as they came ever nearer. They came in one by one making a run over the zone before starting the drop. Food was in wooden boxes, and the medical supplies were to be found in metal canisters. By the time the last plane left with a waggle of its wings we were piling into a wooden box which had been broken open. Then followed perhaps the most wonderful moments of my whole life, when even the captivity that still held us was forgotten. The sight of tinned meats, milk powder, fruit, Bovril, Ovaltine, and endless other good things, gave us a feeling and emotion which we would never enjoy again.

There were a number of womens' camps in the area and we immediately thought of them and their children. I was helping out on one of the vehicles that was taken into a womens' camp; they were at the gates waiting. I shall never forget, nor do I wish to forget, the tears of joy that rolled down the cheeks of emaciated frail women and the pathetic little children. Those children, some of whom could not remember a European nor recognise the piece of chocolate I was handing them, erased from my mind any self-pity I had. I knew at that moment that if ever I should feel capable of forgiving our enemy, which was unlikely, I would never ever forget. We had been through a rough time, but seeing their conditions in a camp on Java left me appalled and forever disgusted with the perpetrators.

Once again those grand Dutch ladies were showing their courage and resolution with heads held high, just as we remembered them from earlier days. I was privileged to have been a relief person able to watch the kiddies' faces as I gave out small pieces of chocolate and sweets. Those moments almost made the suffering seem worth it. Few people are granted such feelings of intense emotion as I experienced then and I am still grateful. Having made our delivery we picked up the lads from the airfield and made our way back to Cycle camp. With a clean body, some new clothing, and food, we sat back on the floor now covered by native straw matting. All of those moments, so difficult to describe, were the most wonderful we would ever know.

An Allied HQ had been set up in a former hotel which I believe was the Des Indies Hotel in Batavia. A staff car had been commandeered, with one or two lads as drivers, to take our senior officers to and from the HQ. On one such trip 'Bull' Brummie (Tom Orton) was the driver, and, in spite of their Jap escort, they were stopped at an Indonesian road-block. They were asked if they were carrying any 'Hollanders', and it was only when assured that all were British that they were allowed to continue. Apparently the insurgents were heavily armed and looked to have been well trained. It was at this HQ that Tom first heard confirmation from Jack Grist about both of my missing friends, Ron Taylor and Bill Pollock. Ron had left Ambon on 1st May 1944, in a party of two hundred that arrived at Java on 21st May 1944. Most of their journey, with Flying Officer Heath in charge, had been spent in the open on the ship's deck as victims of starvation and the tropical heat. Only when a coal bunker became available did the fifty most seriously ill men have some shelter. Fortunately only two men died on this trip, one of starvation. The other, Ron Taylor, was 'murdered'. Ron was a corporal from my own home town of Middlesbrough and our girlfriends were cousins. He was murdered by that infamous Yellow Boots.

This is how Eric Rice remembers the episode.

On 12th May whilst on the Jap hellship *Tencho Maru* between Ambonia and Java, Ron stole some fish from the Japs. He was caught and received a minor bashing. Then the Jap sojo (warrant officer) appeared on the scene and tore a strip off in Japanese that no one understood. Then with the usual Jap contrariness the sojo gave Ron several fish as a 'presento'.

Next day after a short stay in Macassar the sojo came on board drunk. Ron Taylor who was resting in a coal hole with several others believed the incident closed. The coal hole was very hot and always black so the need for fresh air was of paramount importance. Ron left the coal hole by a stairway that led to the upper deck, which was strictly out of bounds to prisoners. Coming back down the stairway he was seen by the sojo who yelled "the thief" and he promptly started beating Taylor with a thick stick. It was deadly quiet and the sounds could be heard all over the very small ship. Judging by those sounds he must have been thrown to the iron deck several times and battered until his body was like pulp. He was more dead than alive when the sojo announced his intention to execute Taylor:

"Has this man any message for his father and mother — I am going to slay him?"

All Taylor could whisper was that he was sorry and he asked the Jap to forgive him and accept his apologies. The sojo then drew his sword and struck a heavy blow on the back of Taylor's neck just below the ear. He followed it up by sticking the point of his sword through the throat, then called on prisoners to throw the body overboard. Someone asked if a prayer could be said — the request was refused. Again the request was made and this time was granted, but the prayer had to be short. Our orderlies (medical) bound the body with sacks taken from home-made stretchers and the body was thrown overboard. What a way to end up; but nothing could have saved him for the Jap was mad drunk amongst some two hundred prisoners, most of whom were too weak to even move in defence.

Imagine the feelings the next day when it was apparent that the same sojo was as drunk as ever. He started off early by lining up the officers, WO's and orderlies, forcing them to sing and dance. Then he grabbed a rifle which most fortunately was not loaded; if it had been he would have shot someone, or everyone. Then for no apparent reason at all he started on an RAF warrant officer. The sojo kicked and punched the prisoner in the face and then wrestled him. It was already evident that the sojo was out for more blood so the warrant officer did the only thing possible — he fought back though by no means fit to do so.

The Jap got the prisoner down and then reached out for some beer bottles which were full of some medicinal liquid and he broke three in rapid succession over the prisoner's head. The prisoner was in a bloody mess from head to foot. Then whilst he was still blinded with the blood, this animal smashed tin food containers into his face. How that prisoner stood up to this treatment I do not know but suddenly he made a run for it and escaped to the top deck where he appealed to the Jap crew for help. Luckily, he met the right chap and was helped, whilst the crew calmed down the sojo. The day wore on with everyone on tenterhooks and then whilst eating our rice meal he appeared yet again with another stick and started wading in amongst our stretcher cases. Again we were lucky; before he could do too much damage, one of the crew came along and persuaded the sojo to leave us alone. For a day or so he was not seen and he remained quiet for the rest of the trip. All the guards were scared stiff of him and always moved away when Yellow Boots was about.

We heard later that he had drowned when with another draft of prisoners en route to Sumatra.

Everyone was pleased to see Java again. It had been a nightmare of a journey. Another man who had got on the wrong side of a guard was roped and thrown overboard to be dragged along behind the ship until the craving of those twisted minds was satisfied. The lad could only be grateful that the sea was then less shark-infested than was usual.

Whilst the insurgents gave us continued cause for concern, many awesome things were taking place outside the camp. Over long periods, the Indonesians had been pushing for their total independence whilst the Japs procrastinated. Since we had arrived back in Java, many changes had taken place both politically and militarily. The culmination of this came one day in early August 1945. A twin-engined bomber appeared from out of the clouds and came low over Kemayoran airfield. No one scattered, no one ran for shelter. Instead the large crowd that had assembled at the airport went wild with joy. The plane came to rest in front of them and a narrow door opened in the side of the fuselage. A figure dressed in a dazzling white suit stood upright in the opening:

'Long live President Soekarno,' came the roar of the crowd,

'Long live merdeka.' (freedom.)

They went wild with enthusiasm as the figure stepped down. He was followed by two others. The Japanese Military Governor of Java, Yamamoto Shigeichi, stepped forward with his greeting. Vigorous handshakes were exchanged and the Japanese, overcome with emotion, began to weep tears of joy. Soekarno came to the dais which had been set up near to the airport buildings. He took a grip on his emotions then mounted the dais and turned to the crowd:

'I told you that Indonesia would be free and independent when the jagon (maize) flower blooms; the jagon has not yet blossomed and we have achieved that independence.'

The crowd went berserk and caps were flung high into the air as thousands of voices yelled themselves hoarse. Under Japanese aegis Indonesia was free at last and colonial rule would never return. Unknown to Soekarno and the screaming crowds, Japan had already accepted the Potsdam declaration and had surrendered unconditionally. Soon the new Republic would begin to look fragile. Indonesia had long been promised their independence, first by Premier Tojo, and again in September 1944 by Koiso.

Japanese procrastination was understandable as Java was the most populated of Japan's conquests in South-East Asia, and, with its tin, rubber and oil, it was one of the richest — it was in order to secure the oilfields in the Dutch East Indies that Japan had made war in the first place. Borneo, Sarawak, Java and Sumatra had been the target of their drive to the south. Their other campaigns in the Philippines, Burma and Malaya, and even the capture of Singapore, were all subsidiary to the securing of fuel for Japan's industry, which the Dutch East Indies provided. Having seized them from the Dutch in a lightning campaign during February and March 1942, Japan was loathe to release them. In Burma and the Philippines, puppet Governments received their Charters of Independence but the Indonesians were kept waiting for theirs. All posts, with the exception of a few at the very top, were in Indonesian hands. But Japan did more than train politicians; she organised an Indonesian military force, using some Indonesians who had been NCO's in the pre-war Royal Netherland Indies army. The Japanese also recruited close on 25,000 troops in Java and 2,000 in Timor called the 'Hei-Ho' (military auxiliaries). It was typical of Japanese military Government to interfere with the most trivial details of the daily lives of their 'people'.

Lieutenant Colonel Laurens Van Der Post had been ordered by Wavell to stay behind in Java in 1942 where he was taken into captivity. He received regular intelligence from Chinese friends outside his prison. Through them he learnt something of the rising tide of nationalism in Java, also, of what the Japanese were said to be planning for the 100,000 Europeans still held in Java. Some officers in the camp managed to construct a secret radio set. This provided Van Der Post with an exact picture of the progress of the war. It also showed him something else which disturbed him profoundly: he had lived in Japan and knew the Japanese well, and he was dismayed that nothing he had heard on the radio offered the Japs what they would regard as an honourable alternative to fighting. According to the logic of their spirit and sense of history, they had to annihilate themselves and all enemy prisoners rather than surrender.

This way of thinking was confirmed by news from a Korean informant, a Christian employed by the Japanese. He reported that a new batch of orders had arrived in May 1945 from Terauchi in Saigon HQ:

'Any notion of defeat or peace by negotiation was rejected, all subordinate commanders were to commit suicide in the traditional Japanese manner, to avoid falling into Allied hands. All prisoners, civilian as well as military, had to be concentrated in Central Java at the hill station of Bandoeng [this would be why we were moved to Bandeong at that time]. When the Allies began their final attack on South East Asia, all prisoners were to be massacred'.

The news of the dropping of the Atomic Bomb (Little Boy) on Hiroshima, which for the rest of the world was the threshold of release from the war, was received by Van Der Post over the secret radio with a mixture of foreboding and optimism. Terauchi and his officers in South East Asia might now take dreadful revenge for Hiroshima on the prisoners in their hands. On the other hand it might conceivably make the prisoners feel they had been the target of something so cataclysmic as to be almost supernatural, which would make them feel able to withdraw from the war without dishonour. Five days later we heard that the Emperor was suing for peace. There were also rumours that the Brisbane-based Dutch had told Mountbatten on 3rd September 1945 that there might be active opposition to the return of the Dutch by the 40,000-odd Republicans on Java. Apart from that they gave no warning of the strength of Nationalist feelings.

Against all the evidence the Brisbane-based Dutch told Mountbatten that the bulk of the population was indifferent to political movements, and that the nationalist movement was the creation of a few individuals only, so occupation would be simple enough once the transport and security problems were overcome. There was a Dutch representative on board HMS *Cumberland* who said the Javanese would welcome the Dutch back. After only one day in port Van Der Plass was obliged to return to the ship for his own safety! When the Japanese came aboard HMS *Cumberland* in Tandjoeng Priok harbour, Batavia, on 15th September 1945, they were told by Admiral Patterson that they had to maintain the status quo until the Allied forces were in position. It would be necessary to use arms to do this and they had to repress any disturbances. Rear Admiral Mida, who had done his best to get the revolution off the ground, was present; to him it was an appalling order. He knew that the disturbances referred to were in effect the Indonesian movement. The Japanese became aware that the Indonesians were carefully watching the stores that were being handed over to the RAPWI.

'Why do Japanese army give to the enemy what it did not give to us, its Allies?' the Indonesians were asking.

The Indonesians began to call at Japanese houses in Batavia demanding that the houses themselves be turned over. They took all weapons belonging to the Jap troops. When a crowd of tens of thousands assembled in Gambir Square in the centre of Batavia for a republican meeting, they were armed to the teeth with Jap weapons and their own mountain knives and bamboo spears. Isolated Japanese detachments were attacked and the Indonesians even grew bold enough to assault the *Kempetai* and take their arms from them. Public buildings in Sourabaya were attacked and women and children were kidnapped as hostages and maltreated; both sides committed abuses. Everyone came under constant harassment from the irregular Indonesian forces. Dutch and Ambonese troops who had landed in spite of Indonesian protests were described as being 'trigger happy' and likely to shoot at anything suspicious. Factions developed within the Jap army as violence and anarchy grew; one faction was for openly disobeying high orders, by staging a mass desertion on behalf of the Indonesians. They thought that all Japs should take weapons and vehicles and join the forces of the Indonesian Republic. This faction believed that their surrender policy had betrayed the Indonesians, so it was now their duty to redeem that betrayal by sacrificing their own lives.

When the Dutch returned to the town of Sourabaya from internment in Central Java, apparently under the auspices of the Japanese, anti-Jap feelings began to run high. On 1st October 1945 the Indonesians attacked important points and seized them by force. A great deal of fighting was taking place in Sourabaya; looters brandishing swords and spears stole and ravished as they fought with the Japanese. Even in West Java, where the Allied control was much stricter, the Japanese managed to hand over large amounts of arms to the Indonesians. The Japanese had also given them something else. When 250,000 Indonesian troops began to struggle against the British and Dutch, they used the tactics which the Japs assured them had been the secret of success against Western forces — they attacked by night. Mountbatten deployed two British Indian Divisions in Java alone, and some forces were cut to pieces. There were many cases of Japs being ambushed by the Indonesians and Japanese civilians being massacred.

The Bekasi incident is one example of this. Over eighty Japanese soldiers *en route* from Bekasi for defence duties were stopped by about six hundred Indonesian youths as they approached the iron bridge near Bekasi. The youths demanded their arms and one Japanese called out:

'We are carrying no arms.'

The youths made them all stand in a row to be searched and they discovered two officers carried revolvers.

'Why did you lie?' they yelled angrily.

Before the Japanese could explain the order came:

'Finish them off'.

All eighty were killed with bamboo spears and their bodies were thrown under the bridge.

Similarly, at Semerang about seventy-nine Japanese were staffing an army transport office; they had women and children with them. On the night of 14th October 1945, they were forced to line up in their night attire outside the office gates. Taken to the police station at nearby Baru they were searched, beaten and packed into a cell 'like rice in a bag' as the Japanese would put it. They were given no food or drink throughout the night, and no means of relieving themselves. In the midst of choking heat, the stench of their cell was soon indescribable. They spent the whole day in that cell until about midnight on the 15th when ten extremists armed with pistols and rifles appeared.

'The Japanese must die!' they shouted angrily.

They began calling the men out one by one, and shooting them. Those who remained in the cell protested, so the Indonesians turned the guns upon them and deluged the cell with rifle fire. Every one of those Japanese died. The story goes that one of them, before he died, wrote on the wall of the cell in his own blood:

'Baha giya Indonesia merdeka.' (Glory to the freedom of Indonesia.)

These words are apparently preserved on that cell wall in remembrance of the friendship between Japan and Indonesia. It is quite feasible that a Jap about to die might have foreseen the day when 'merdeka' would not lead to massacre, and he had magnanimously forgiven his murderers. It is also feasible that in his death throes he may have scrawled the words in bitter mortal irony. Either way the conjunction of Japanese death and Indonesian freedom was the reality.

Over a period of six weeks we in Cycle camp became aware that in the east of the island much fighting was now taking place. Each day we envisaged the mob outside being provided with arms; nothing could then have saved our skins. We were indeed fortunate that the grip on West Java was that much tighter than in the east, Sourabaya in particular. If we had needed more to worry about it would have been for those of our own kind who were now cut off at the other end of the island. Our return to Java from the islands of Ambon and Haruku may not have been such a good move after all, but such is fate. My God, how we prayed someone would get us out and fast, our luck couldn't hold forever.

On 13th September 1945, we were told that we could now write home to our loved ones. The messages would get top priority, we were told by a visiting VIP from Singapore.

'All arrangements possible are being made to get you all out as soon as we are able; your situation is known outside of Java.'

That received the loudest cheer our friend had ever heard, at least for some time. The last time my family had heard from me must have been in 1942/3 from the Jaarmarkt camp. At that time we had been allowed a few standard words such as:

"Do not worry, I'm being 'looked after'," on a Japanese postcard — not too many of them reached England.

A message was received from HMS *Cumberland* which said:

'Prepare those most ill for passage out on this ship to Singapore; others will leave by air and those most fit will remain until the last.'

'Just my luck,' I thought. Why had I been so grateful to those on the staff at St Vincentous Hospital? Of course I knew I did appreciate their care for me, but right then I wished to be just a little indisposed until I was out of Java.

Our officers who had these decisions to make did it well and with the utmost fairness. Wing Commander Jack Carlyle was one of the last to leave, as was our staunch officer and friend Squadron Leader Pitts, who delayed his return home so as to help RAPWI, and also give evidence to the War Crimes Tribunal. It was a mark of unselfishness and a determination to see justice done on behalf of those we had to leave behind, forever. Not all Japs could be treated as war criminals; some had only handed out the same punishments they themselves were liable to receive in accordance with their codes. It was mainly the barbaric, treacherous and sadistic ones, who had exposed us to a violent slavery and thoroughly enjoyed doing so, that needed to be brought to justice. They had deliberately destroyed the dignity of men before literally starving them to death, and I repeat again, *so unnecessarily*. We had no compunction whatsoever about the fate of the likes of Yellow Boots, Mori and Kasiyama or commandants like Kurishima and Sonai of Cycle camp infamy. Those and many others were not fit to live amongst decent people; they had made our every day a hell on earth for 1,316 days, or if you prefer 30,158 long hours.

In a day or two we were to leave behind those screaming mobs. The last of the so-called fit had been drafted (yet again) on to a Jap ship, and not on to the promised aircraft. The situation was becoming so intense and serious that it was decided we could wait no longer and arrangements were made to commandeer the ship in the harbour of Tandjoeng Priok. What an irony to travel again in a Jap ship, but this time I was never happier. Thank goodness the MS *Sumire Maru* would have a British captain and no more watery soup or rice 'pap'. The ship was to be crewed by Japs and Indonesians with two British officers and a number of naval ratings in charge. That was the best and last journey I ever intended to make on a Jap ship. However, these people had still not quite finished with us; there were to be one or two parting traumas.

Under an armed guard of Japanese we left the camp gates to negotiate a rather scary journey through the district to the docks, never sure if we would be stopped and attacked. Then, after having set sail on the *Sumire Maru*, the Jap crew attempted two or three times to set fires on board. They had to be watched carefully by the good old matloes until we reached Keppal harbour three days later, to the most wonderful of sounds that finally told us:

'You are now free and amongst your friends, welcome home.'

The hooters of dozens of ships seeing our approach were letting it rip for all they were worth! It was truly fantastic and I cried, quietly.

It was yet another wonderful feeling to simply walk the streets of Singapore a 'free man' able to watch the enemy 'at work' under our guards. One feature, however, still puzzled me and I still failed to understand why: *they had not committed Hara-Kiri.*

Apart from the one or two real fanatics who kept their word and so-called 'honour', no one else had seen or heard of any other ritual suicides. The conditions they were being worked under were correct; not many of us would have had it any other way now that we were free. Had we perpetrated further their evil deeds, then we would have been no better than them, the people we had learnt to hate. We must hope that they have learnt a lesson but I have very grave doubts.

We were placed in a building called Sea View Mansions, whilst others remained on the *Sumire Maru* or on the ship we would travel home on, the MV *Celecia*. Everything seemed so wonderful, and so important, that it felt like wonderland, and I suppose it was true when it was said that we were all acting a little odd. Naturally one fellow strutted around with a real cocky pride and his RAF ceremonial hat set at just the correct angle. That hat he married in, was taken prisoner in and freed in; I expect now he will be gardening in it. Who else but Tommy the Brummie Bull could be so proud of his RAF connection?

On about 20th October 1945, we were put aboard the MV *Celecia*, a rather nice ship and luxury for us. Soon we steamed west across the Indian Ocean towards the Suez Canal. During the voyage we were given the very best of food (regulated), vitamins and one pint of beer each day. Those still carrying malaria symptoms in their bloodstream were treated with a new drug, mepequine; the quinine we craved for was now out of fashion.

This journey would be much quicker and shorter than when we left England in 1941. We were quickly becoming different men, the flesh was being filled as though a balloon, and our 'dulled' senses were awakening. We began to be our true selves again and were asking: 'Had this all really happened?'

We arrived at Port Tewfick and as we approached the quayside we could see a large banner: 'Welcome home boys!' It was accompanied by a military band. My final and lasting memory of four lost years was of those people on the quayside at Liverpool who held aloft a large white linen bed sheet on which it said: 'Welcome home Tom Vigurs.' I suspect, along with Tom Vigurs, ex-Harukean, that we all enjoyed that particular welcome back into Blighty; it was about the only one we received until we each arrived in our own home.

We all moved into RAF Cosford for a quick medical, far too quick for those who were left to suffer for many years afterwards in the hands of medical personnel who knew little or nothing of tropical medicine! This was followed by a de-briefing, after which we couldn't get home quickly enough; the authorities were only too glad to agree.

After the Christmas of 1945 many of us returned for demobbing and to say our last farewell and goodbye's to each other before taking up a normal life once more— already some felt it was going to be an unexciting one! Less than 40% of my friends in 242 Squadron had been known to survive their battle; many more died later and too soon after their experiences. So if a friend should ask you:

'Why is it that some Far East Prisoners of War (Fepow's) can forgive their captors — yet most cannot forget?', may I suggest that you ask them to read this story, our story, then perhaps they will understand.

> Life, no matter how conceived
> Has to be the most wonderful of gifts
> Given to each only once
> Life, is ours for the betterment
> Of all good, not evil.

> If I hated a newborn Japanese child
> I would be no better than those I condemn
> We should not hate, nor
> Should we forget.

Anon.

Appendices

Justice

The following is the experience of an aide to the Provost Marshal during the execution of War Criminals found to be guilty.

'Yesterday, I saw a sight that no doubt many ex-Pows from Jap camps would have given a lot to see. In between 9.00am and 10.30am I saw eight war criminals pay for their crimes at the end of a rope. The prisoners were eight Jap naval officers and ratings who had been ordered to take eight hundred prisoners and maroon them on an island in the Nicobar group, an island without food or water. They carried out the order to the letter but added to it by throwing two hundred overboard in deep water, laughing whilst they drowned. Another twenty or thirty were severely beaten, out of which only sixteen survived. Retribution came yesterday morning at Changi jail in the north-eastern corner of Singapore Island, a place that itself had seen many Jap criminals.

I was detailed to act as the provost marshal's aide at the execution. The PM is the officer who is responsible for carrying out all military executions and therefore must be present. I met him at our HQ on one of the most beautiful mornings I had ever seen, and as we drove along the coast road through glorious scenery I wondered just how the Japs would be feeling. Life never felt so good to me after being so near to death; I really appreciated it. We arrived at the jail and after being led through several gates we went to the governor's office where we collected the death warrants.

We then made our way to the gallows in the company of the governor, and I must say they were not quite like the ones I had visualised after reading detective stories. They were like a Tote Indicator at the dog races, a tall wooden building with a corrugated roof. There was a top floor open all round with a rail rather like a balcony at about 25 feet from the ground. It differed from a balcony, however, because in the centre of the floor was a large trap door controlled by a large lever, rather like a railway points lever. Above this trap was a beam from which hung three short lengths of chain, and from each chain hung a white rope. At the end of each rope was a large loop bound in cloth, not the conventional hangman's knot but an ordinary slip knot. Underneath the trap was a large room with big doors which were wide open so that anybody at ground level could see the bodies drop through. The whole building was situated in the prison yard. Leading up to the gallows was a long carpeted ramp from a small door in the inside wall; this led to a corridor leading from the condemned cells.

The party in the dress circle consisted of the PM, myself, two executioners and the governor of the jail. The hangmen were British prison officials and really looked the part; they had been interned by the Japs and had no particular love for them. When we arrived they were busy working out the length of drop required for each man, the smaller the man the longer the drop.

At 9am the PM nodded to me and the whole party proceeded down the ramp and through the small door. Inside there were guards and an interpreter. We stopped at the first cell and the jailer opened the door. A Jap was sitting reading as we entered, and he stood up, bowed, and wished us good morning. The interpreter read out the death warrant and asked if he had any last request to make. He merely thanked us for looking after him so well and asked that we return his books to the library. He didn't turn a hair and treated the whole matter as a joke. The executioner then strapped his hands behind his back and placed the hood over his head. He was then stood outside in the corridor whilst two others were also prepared. When they were all lined up we led them through the door and up the ramp. I led the first one and the executioners led the others. My Jap said in English,

'Thank you very much, goodbye.'

I think I murmured something like,

'Not at all, it's my pleasure.'

The executioner had marked out three places with names on the trap and they were stood on them whilst the executioner placed the ropes around their necks. I helped to strap their legs together. As soon as we had strapped them up they all started to shout the Jap battle cry 'Banzai!' at the top of their voices. It was really a terrible sound and seemed to fill the prison yard. Then the executioner told us to stand back, and looked at the PM. The PM nodded and the executioner pulled the lever. Everything seemed to happen in a flash. One second there were three hooded and strapped Japs yelling on the trap. The next second there was a terrible crash as the traps dropped open and the three bodies were catapulted into open space still yelling. Then came the snap of three ropes suddenly being jerked tight and for a split second there was complete silence as though they had all held their breath. Then three bodies gently swung at the end of their ropes with not a twitch or a move. I looked closely at their hands from above but there was not even a quiver, they never knew what had hit them. The executioner leant forward and felt the rope to see if any tremors were running through their bodies, looked at me and said

'That was a nice drop.'

The tension was broken and everyone pulled out cigarettes and began to talk whilst the bodies hung for the prescribed fifteen minutes. After fifteen minutes the medical party pulled a platform up to the bodies and the MO stood on it to test their hearts to see if they were dead — they were. They were cut down and dumped on a litter with the hood removed. Their faces looked quite normal but rather purple and there was no expression of pain. The neck had a deep red weal around it and was distorted, obviously broken. The chief executioner looked down through the trap and said with a touch of professional pride, 'Nice break'.

I don't think anybody felt either sympathy or malice for them; the whole business was just regarded as a job. I personally felt it was nothing but an experience. The trap was hauled up again and fresh ropes were fixed. Three more Japs were led out and exactly the same performance was repeated, including the 'Banzai'. After two more we went back to the governor's office and signed the 'sentence carried out' portion of the warrant. Though I hold no grief for the Japs I will say they died like men, without a whimper. They must be fanatics, though, to stand on a trap with ropes around their necks on the brink of eternity and yell 'Banzai'.

That was all there was to it; we drove home and the morning seemed, if anything, nicer than before. I expect now that my name is on their list of war criminals so I will have to watch out if we have another war with them! It was an unusual experience and I regard it as such . . .'

Those hanged were real criminals and I couldn't help but hope that the next four in turn would be Mori, Yellow Boots, Kasiyama and Kurishima, then I would know there was such a thing as 'true justice'.

A Christian in the Enemy's House

The 'Christian' was the Korean soldier working in the Japanese Military Intelligence who was already in contact with Laurens Van Der Post at the time the *Maros Maru* was heading for Java. The contact had been arranged by friends (Chinese) of Van Der Post, who were still on the outside.

The informant told of hundreds of prisoners who had died on Haruku through the inefficient system of logistics, and the brutality carried out by the Japs. He also told of those coming back, travelling in the most terrible conditions, saying that many would not survive the journey. He further warned Van Der Post that the guards who were mainly responsible for the worst of the atrocities on Haruku were returning to take up high ranking positions in prisoner of war camps on Java.

Laurens Van Der Post once said,

'I think none of us who saw the day that his story came true could possibly ever forget it.'

The few survivors who came into camp looked like pictures of the last inmates of Belsen on their day of liberation. The story of their journey from Haruku (Ambon as well) to Java was in every way as terrible as my Korean informant had predicted.

Among the survivors was a Royal Air Force officer I had known well, yet I did not recognise him until he spoke his name, 'Blackwood'. He did so in a voice which I could hardly hear. Blackwood told me of the sea journey when his men had died so fast that they were thrown over the side at a rate of seventeen to twenty-seven *a day*.

The worst of the guards appeared on the staff of our own camp, like the unbelievable *Gunso* Mori and his Korean satellite — a tiny man of unlimited energy, resource and variety of mood; a complete mixture of extreme sadistic impulses and unpredictable generosity, who had adopted the Japanese name of Kasiyama, and who was later condemned to death by a war crimes tribunal. He was to hang side by side with his Japanese overlord — *Gunso* Mori.

James Home
RAF
Java
14th September 1945

All at home
The devil has thrown away his fork and I am free (almost); neither he nor I know how this was possible. I am waiting to be taken out, perhaps to Singapore then home — it's almost unbelievable. Although I never lost faith the odds have been terrific. However, it is over now and the difficult task of forgetting is to be faced. I am quite the artisan now; I can live 'almost' to perfection the life of the lowest native. Blood, sweat and toil throughout the world has paved the way to 'happier' days. I know of no address for a reply, I hope to be on the high seas by the time this gets home. I will inform you whenever possible. We started off with fourteen 'local' lads and now five are left . . . etc.

Till soon
Jimmy

22.9.1945
Saturday

Forgive me if I seem to make this letter short. Why, I don't know, but somehow I just cannot express my emotions. Today I returned from a relief party in a women's camp. For pigs, let alone females, the conditions were appalling, almost unbelievable. God forbid that my sisters ever see such conditions or be subjected to it — the swines. Sorry to relate we have not been excused these atrocities; all who oppose the Japs cannot evade it.

Myself I am now quite well but for some awful memories. You seemed to think I am on my way home; wait patiently for I am still not any nearer. Don't worry it is only a matter of time. Yet here we cannot understand what is meant by the statement, 'Highest priority for prisoners.'

Five weeks have passed since VJ day, yet still we sit in Java with 60,000 armed pigs and no sign of occupation. The Yanks and Aussies are flying out but as usual the Bulldog waits until the end.

Every day a new Big Noise (all red tape) arrives by air, each with a different idea, so here we are, only about eight hundred of us left in Java. But we expect relief any time now; providing the position is the same we may hear something to our advantage.

Give my love to the boys and Eleanor. I remain anxious to renew my experiences of a good dinner at 89, as at Olive's.

Soon for Ayresome, Bill.

Cheerio
Jim.

Middlesbrough
Yorkshire
19th November 1945

Dear Tom (Elgey)

Boy was I glad to hear from you, for obvious reasons I did not dare write to your home — just in case. I must excuse myself for not having replied sooner, the fact is I took your letter to Ron Taylor's family for their perusal. Already I was in touch with Ron's folk because he and I were pretty big friends. I had told them pretty well the same story, having got it from Jack Grist at the Jap HQ in Batavia.

Gee, Tom it is good to know you are back and now reasonably well. How are you finding life — grumbling because the steak is a little under done?

I was disappointed when I found you had gone from Java — I got back last December ('44), totally paralysed from the waist down but only physically not mentally. I spent all my time from early '43 until a year ago playing builders on Haruku, Ambon and the Celebes (Macassar). On the way back from Ambon to Java, the boat, although a sick draft, was stopped at Macassar by intense Allied activity. Typically Jap; whilst in port working parties started on demolition work. That was the straw that broke this camel's back, and beriberi began to take control of arms, hands and legs. Enough of that, it seems impossible now that we ordinary mortals could survive. No one is more proud than I of the matchless Bulldog breed.

Today I went out and bought myself a new set of civvies. Can you imagine me staying in after the heartache of these last four years? No siree, I have got myself a girlfriend and a job with the GPO Engineers, all ready for the plunge. I return to Cosford on the 9th December so we will have a run in and see the Wolves. Here's hoping everyone at your home is as you would wish. Give my respects to all and until Hell freezes

Your old pal Jim.

During the November of 1945, having reached home and met with my friend Tom Elgey again, I asked him to drop a line to Joe Parkers' mother (I chickened out, emotionally). Joe's mum was living in Suffolk. It was agreed to play down any talk or real hardships and cruelty and have his mum think his death was due to tropical disease alone. This is an extract from his mother's reply.

> 15 Council Houses
> Snape
> Nr Saxmundham
> Suffolk
> 20.11.1945

Dear Sergeant Elgey

Thank you so very much for your great kindness in writing to me about my darling Joey. Thank God he did not suffer much as I have always thought he might have been beaten by the Japs or something like that. We had only one small card on which Joey's age was given as 20 and it reached me when he was nearly 23. God bless you dear boy for writing to me.

You have lifted a load from my mind about how Joey died and I am so glad he was a good friend to the last. When you are feeling better yourself will you write to me again and tell me if Joey ever got any of my letters and cards. I wrote to him every week although we were supposed to write only once a fortnight. My son loved his mother and would do anything for me so my loss is almost more than I can bear but I try to think he is better off, but we all loved him so. Tell your dear mother I know how she must feel but thank God she got you back again. I hope you understand my scribble but please excuse me as my head has been so funny since I received the telegram saying Joey had died, we always thought he would just walk in on us.

> Yours very sincerely
> M Parker

Every word of feeling in that letter was like a knife in my heart — for I, too, thought the world of Joe — like my brother, I still miss him.

A short retrospect from my good friend Martin.

News from Home

In the depressing days on Haruku island during 1943, spirits of the POW were raised a little in October of that year when a rumour spread that some mail had arrived at the camp. Typically the Nips held on to the letters for some days before allowing them to be distributed. Fortunate recipients hastily opened theirs, but there were many men for whom there was nothing and they sat back in the shadows hiding their feelings. Many letters could not be delivered since the addressees had lain in the cemetery for many weeks. News from home was scanty and very old, my letter being dated June 1942. The usual question asked by friends was,

'Is everything OK with your people?'

One man was puzzled as to the sentiment intended when he read

'Glad to hear you are a POW.'

But the prize comment came from a lugubrious pigeon fancier from the West Ridings. 'Yorkie' sat on the edge of the *bali-bali* staring at his letter with an expression more morose than usual:

'Aye' he said, 'I knew the folks would be alright but it says nowt about mi birds.'

Sincere good wishes
Martin Ofield.

Martin was a lucky one — I never ever received any word, like so many more.

The 'Fepow' Prayer

As we that are left grow old with the years
Remembering the heartaches, the pain and the tears
Hoping and praying that never again
Will man sink to such sorrow and shame
The price that was paid — we will always remember
Every day, every month — not just in November.

Amen.

The Kohima Epitaph

The words of a dying soldier to a pal trying to comfort him:

When you go home, tell them of us
For your tomorrow we gave our today.